Plymouth
On This Day

Plymouth
On This Day

Rick Cowdery

Plymouth
On This Day

Pitch Publishing Ltd
A2 Yeoman Gate
Yeoman Way
Durrington
BN13 3QZ

Email: info@pitchpublishing.co.uk
Web: www.pitchpublishing.co.uk

First published in the UK by Pitch Publishing, 2014
Text © 2014 Rick Cowdery

ISBN: 978-1-909626-67-6
Cover design: Brilliant Orange Creative Services.
Typesetting: Alan Wares.
Editor: Dan Tester www.copymatters.co.uk
Printed in Great Britain. Production managed by Jellyfish Solutions.

DEDICATION

For my Mum.

ACKNOWLEDGEMENTS

I am indebted, yet again, to Mike Curno, who has added another string to his already overstrung bow by taking the photographs within – he and Alec Henderson also did the proofreading – as well as helping with the research (plenty of which came from his own experiences). Like Mike said, you cannot unearth anything already unearthed, so I am grateful for those keen historians of Plymouth who have gone before me.

I referred, and refer you, to the following publications: A Century of Plymouth, Guy Fleming, Sutton Publishing; Chronicle of Britain, ed. Henrietta Heald, Jol International Publishing; Chronicle of the Royal Family, ed. Derrik Mercer, Chronicle Communications Ltd; A Guide to the Archives Department of Plymouth City Libraries, Corporation of Plymouth; 100 Years of the Herald, James Mildren, Bossiney Books; Images of Plymouth, Tom Bowden, Sutton Publishing; It Came to Our Door, HP Twyford, revised by Chris Robinson, Pen & Ink Publishing; Plymouth in Pictures, Crispin Gill, David & Charles; Plymouth's Historic Barbican, Chris Robinson, Pen & Ink Publishing; Plymouth Yesterday, Vic Saundercock, Vic Saundercock; Vanishing Plymouth, Brian Moseley, BS Moseley; A Walk Around St Andrew's the Mother Church of Plymouth, Crispin Gill; Water From the Moor, David J Hawkings, Devon Books. I also spent many hours marvelling at the following websites: www.chrisrobinson.co.uk/pages/index.shtml; www.cyber-heritage.co.uk (Steve Johnson); www.leighrayment.com; www.localhistories.org/plymouth.html (Tim Lambert); www.nationalarchives.gov.uk; www.plymouth.gov.uk; www.plymouthdata.info (Brian Moseley); plymouthlocalhistory.blogspot.com (Derek Tait). Also, grateful thanks to the team at Pitch Publishing for helping me complete a hat-trick in their colours.

Rick Cowdery – 2014

FOREWORD

From the Hoe to edge of Dartmoor; from the days of Drake to the achievements of Daley; from a regal and important past to future of endless possibilities, Plymouth is a city of brilliant and hugely enjoyable contrasts.

I am not a Plymothian, but, if I was, I know I would be proud to call it home, and there are thousands, past and present, who feel exactly the same way. Some of the reasons why – the places and the people; the eras and the events – are contained in the following pages.

This book recalls Plymouth's rich and vibrant history, which has played a huge role in the development of this country, not to mention the world: the first non-indigenous citizens of America, Australia and New Zealand all set out for their new worlds from Plymouth. You are reminded of the city's people, who have often been just colourful – Plymouth has given the world pirates and Parliamentarians; artists and Admirals of the Fleet; heroes and historians; mariners, Pilgrims, explorers, Olympians; and many others. Surnames alone are evocative enough: Carver, Drake, Hawkins, Raleigh, Smeaton, MacBride, Astor, Foot, Scott, Owen, Cook, Lenkiewicz, Francis, Davies, Daley, to name but a few.

Then there are the memorable places in and around the city: Devonport Dockyard, of course; the Hoe; Freedom Fields; the Barbican; Mount Batten; the Breakwater; Mutley Plain; Stonehouse Creek; and more besides. And, the events that helped shape Plymouth and, subsequently, the world: the building of the Dockyard; the sailing of the *Mayflower*; the English Civil War; the World War II blitz; the post-war reconstruction. All these, and much, much, more, are contained in this book, which does not try so much to re-draw Plymouth's history, as to draw it together in daily, bite-sized chunks which should satisfy any appetite.

Enjoy your daily visit to a wonderful city.

James Brent
Owner and Chairman, Plymouth Argyle
Chairman and CEO, Akkeron Group LLP

INTRODUCTION

Right. Cards on the table. I'm not a Plymothian. However, I have been lucky enough to have called Plymouth 'home' for 28 years, during which time I have worked exclusively at the hub of two of its major institutions – the *Western Morning News* and Plymouth Argyle. I therefore think I enjoy the best of both worlds; I am able to view the city and its surrounds as an outsider, but an outsider who has plenty of inside knowledge.

I wrote 'lucky' in the second sentence, and I meant it. Plymouth is a magnificent city. I honestly believe many Plymothians do not appreciate just how magnificent. I hope, if this modest little tome achieves anything, it is to rekindle their passion and pride for Plymouth.

Until Hitler laid waste to it, Plymouth was one of the leading cities in the world, never mind in this country. Actually, Plymouth arguably peopled the world. The cosmopolitan populations of modern-day USA, Australia and New Zealand had their beginnings on the quayside of the Barbican.

The Plymouth of Drake, Hawkins, Frobisher, Raleigh, Nelson, Reynolds, Scott, Gibbons, the Foots, and the Astors, to name only a few of the city's residents, is something of which to be very proud. They represent a glorious past which can yet help shape the future.

Nor am I a historian. If you want to discover the depths of Plymouth's marvellous adolescence, read one of the many books/websites/labours of love fashioned by the splendid Chris Robinson, Brian Moseley, Steve Johnson, Guy Fleming, Tom Bowden, Crispin Gill or Derek Tait. If it has happened in Plymouth, one or all of them will have it lovingly covered in the fullest detail.

No, this is not a history book to be pored over. It is a fun book to dip into – on a daily basis, if you will – which celebrates wonderful Plymouth and her considerable, formidable, brilliant Plymothians. A city and a people of which to be proud.

Rick Cowdery – January 2014

ABOUT THE AUTHOR

Once upon a time, like most journalists, Rick Cowdery thought it would be 'nice to write a book', just so he could tell his grandchildren he was 'an author'. *Plymouth On This Day* is Rick's tenth book, and poor little Ellie May's going to get a right ear-bashing when she is old enough.

Previously, former *Western Morning News* sports editor Rick has penned biographies of Plymouth Argyle personalities Tommy Tynan, Neil Warnock, Paul Sturrock and Paul Wotton, as well as working with Pitch Publishing on *Plymouth Argyle Miscellany* and *Plymouth Argyle On This Day*. Do you see a theme?

Since leaving the *Western Morning News* in 2003, Rick has worked for Plymouth Argyle Football Club as the club's Head of Communications.

JANUARY

THURSDAY 1st JANUARY 1824

Devonport, one of the 'Three Towns' that would later merge to form the city of Plymouth, came into being. Locals living in Plymouth Dock – often shortened to just 'Dock' – were miffed that the name of their town sounded like they were a bolt-on to Plymouth, which was actually smaller. So they petitioned King George IV to allow it to be changed, and the First Gentleman of Europe, being a gentleman, granted them their wish. A little over 104 years later, the city of Plymouth resulted from a not universally welcomed amalgamation of the two county boroughs of Devonport and Plymouth and the sandwiched urban district of East Stonehouse. Even when the trio were united as a county borough in 1914, they still retained some individual identity by being referred to collectively as 'The Three Towns'.

FRIDAY 1st JANUARY 1993

Independent television station, Westcountry TV, began broadcasting to Plymouth. The first offering from the new broadcasters was a welcome by voiceover veterans Bruce Hammal and Trish Bertram that promised higher levels of regional output. This immediately preceded the film *Best Defense*, made in Hollywood and set in America and Kuwait.

MONDAY 1st JANUARY 2007

Professor Roland Levinsky, vice-chancellor of the University of Plymouth since 2002, died when he was electrocuted while enjoying a New Year's Day walk near his house in Wembury. A gust of wind blew down overhead power cables, one of which fatally touched him. An arts building at the university, which opened in September 2007, was named in his honour and a memorial fund was established in his name. Under his direction, the University of Plymouth had climbed 33 places to 40th in *The Guardian* newspaper's ranking of the best British universities.

TUESDAY 2nd JANUARY 1973

The first Brittany Ferries ferry ferried ferry-passengers from Millbay Docks. Brittany Ferries' inaugural journey was between Plymouth and the Breton port of Roscoff, a route which remains England's westernmost Channel crossing, although it is not still served by the ferry that operated that first run, MV *Kérisnel*. Since 2008, more than 400,000 passengers a year have travelled between Plymouth and Roscoff.

FRIDAY 3rd JANUARY 1718

Many different newspapers, some in a variety of guises, have reported on happenings and events in the city of Plymouth and beyond. The first was the *Plymouth Weekly Journal*, or *General Post*, which first hit the news-stands in the second decade of the 18th century. William Kent was the publisher of the *Journal*, printed in Southside Street, which sold for one-and-a-half pence and was really just a reprint of items from the nationals. The oldest issue still in existence – held at the British Library – is dated 5th September, 1718.

TUESDAY 3rd JANUARY 1860

The *Western Morning News* newspaper was first published in Plymouth by Edward Spender and William Saunders. It was printed more or less continuously in the city until April 2010, when the presses were moved to Oxfordshire.

FRIDAY 4th JANUARY 1740

Captain Robert Fanshawe, Member of Parliament for Plymouth between 1784 and 1790, was born. He entered the Royal Navy when barely a teenager and was promoted to captain at the age of 28. A strict disciplinarian, but respected for his seamanship and courage, he saw action in various parts of the world before retiring from service in 1783. He represented Plymouth at Westminster for seven years, after which he was appointed Commissioner of Plymouth Dockyard. He stood down from that post in 1815, having, according to a no-doubt hagiographic family history, borne: "A principal share of the duty of equipping and supplying the British Navy during the greatest crisis of its existence."

SATURDAY 5th JANUARY 1856

The *William Hammond*, a barque which transported convicts to Western Australia, departed Plymouth. Under the captaincy of Horatio Edwards, she sailed with 250 convicts among her 348 passengers, as well as 32 crew, and arrived in Fremantle 84 days later. The major incident on the voyage came three weeks into the journey when chief mate David Kid was discovered drunk on his watch, having taken advantage of the *William Hammond*'s stores of rum without permission. Before sailing, the hapless Kid had been attacked by another sailor, John Deady, who was tried before a Plymouth magistrate and sentenced to 21 days' imprisonment.

FRIDAY 6th JANUARY 2006

The master of a coaster was fined £2,000 by Plymouth magistrates after pleading guilty to endangering life. Ukrainian Yuri Moskalenko, 40, was also ordered to pay £1,500 costs over an incident in the Dover Strait earlier in the year. Magistrates heard how he constantly altered the course of the Panamanian-registered *Dreamer 1* for nearly three hours, manoeuvres described by the Coastguard as "the most dangerous incident in the English Channel for nearly 30 years". *Dreamer 1* had left King's Lynn with a cargo of scrap bound for Plymouth before suffering a steering gear failure, whereupon Moskalenko deemed it "safer" to continue, rather than stop to sort out the problem.

MONDAY 7th JANUARY 2002

British Airways permanently grounded their daily route to Paris from Plymouth City Airport, claiming unacceptable losses by the service, which also called in at Jersey. Rivals British European Airways responded by promoting its flights to the Channel Islands from Exeter.

SUNDAY 8th JANUARY 1978

Plymouth Zoo at Barn Park was closed due to lack of interest and transformed into a skateboard park. However, a quarantine facility – for animals, rather than skateboarders – stayed in operation for several more years. The zoo was adjacent to Plymouth Argyle's Home Park, and it was not unknown for errant footballs to need recovering from animals' pens.

WEDNESDAY 8th JANUARY 1701

Brigadier-General Henry Trelawny died, one day shy of a year after being elected Member of Parliament for Plymouth. Henry was a British Army officer of Cornish descent, the seventh and youngest son of Sir Jonathan Trelawny. At the time of his by-election triumph, Plymouth returned two MPs, and the city's other parliamentary representative was Henry's brother Charles, who sat from 1698 to 1713.

SATURDAY 9th JANUARY 1841

George Hobbs, a gunner on HMS *Pigeon*, was hung from the yardarm of a ship moored in the Hamoaze – the stretch of water where the Rivers Tamar, Tavy, and Lynher meet – having been convicted of being drunk on duty and striking an officer; presumably the one who discovered him drunk on duty.

THURSDAY 10th JANUARY 1929

Wildlife celeb Dr Tony Soper was born in Plymouth. A graduate of Devonport High School, he co-founded the BBC's Natural History Unit and produced the Beeb's first full-length wildlife film, *The Fulmar*, about the fulmar petrel, naturally, in 1958. Five years later, he became Johnny Morris's sidekick in *Animal Magic* and went on to present *Nature* on BBC2. The presenter, script-writer and author – he has written more than a dozen books – has also been awarded an honorary doctorate from the University of Plymouth.

TUESDAY 10th JANUARY 1995

The Edgcumbe Arms pub at Cremyll, which dates back to the 15th century, was reopened by the Earl of Mount Edgcumbe – his local – 11 months after being burnt to a shell. The fire had little effect on the original stone-flagged floors but was a little less forgiving to the historical oak beams.

SATURDAY 11th JANUARY 1941

An unexploded nine-foot long one-ton bomb, the biggest that fell on Plymouth during World War II, was removed from a house in Wolsdon Street. Legend has it that the explosive behemoth fell through the kitchen floor while the home-owners were in their shelter; on returning to the house, they were unaware of its presence beneath them and slept there for several nights before the bomb was found.

SATURDAY 12th JANUARY 1788

Plymouth was 'all alive by the presence' of George, Prince of Wales (later King George IV), and his younger brother, Frederick, Duke of York, according to a report in *The Times*. Their Royal Highnesses were in town to visit another brother, William, who, later in life, succeeded George to the throne. William had joined the Navy as a 13-year-old and, amongst other postings, served under Horatio Nelson in the West Indies.

TUESDAY 13th JANUARY 1846

The Plymouth Health of Towns Association was formed by Liberal town councillor George Soltau after a public meeting at the Mechanics' Institute in Princess Square. At the time, Plymouth was one of Britain's most unhealthy towns with an infant mortality-rate that meant 25 per thousand would die before their first birthday.

TUESDAY 14th JANUARY 1941

Luftwaffe raids seriously deprived swathes of the city of gas and electricity as the Plymouth and Stonehouse Gas Company in Cattedown was badly damaged and the Plymouth Corporation Electricity Power House was put out of action. The *Western Morning News* was printed in Exeter as the German bombs had halted operations in Frankfort Gate. Typesetters, technicians and journalists were ferried by taxis to the *Express and Echo* plant to carry on production of the paper, which was duly delivered to breakfast tables with readers barely any the wiser as to the problems encountered getting it there.

SATURDAY 15th JANUARY 1944

General Bernard Montgomery lent his considerable military weight to the opening of Plymouth Merchant Navy Week by the Lord Mayor of London, Sir Frank Newson-Smith. Monty was back in Blighty to take command of the 21st Army Group, which consisted of Allied ground forces that would take part in Operation Overlord, the invasion of Normandy. He was back in town a few months later, visiting the Dockyard.

THURSDAY 16th JANUARY 1873

Ivor Guest, Member of Parliament for Plymouth between 1900 and 1906, was born. After following Winston Churchill and other fellow Conservatives into the Liberal Party in support of free trade, he was ennobled as Lord Wimborne and went on to become one of the last Lords-Lieutenant of Ireland, serving in that position at the time of the Easter Rising.

WEDNESDAY 16th JANUARY 1929

Dame Sophia Gertrude Wintz, co-founder of the Royal Sailors' Rests, died. The Swiss-born philanthropist and her friend Agnes Weston started holding Sunday afternoon meetings for boys from training ships at Devonport at Wintz's mother's house, later buying a pub in Plymouth and replacing it with a Sailors' Rest for all nationalities on shore leave. They also set up: the Royal Naval Temperance Society; the journals *Monthly Letters* and *Ashore and Afloat*; and a library that distributed literature to ships all over the world. Wintz, who was appointed Dame Commander of the Order of the British Empire in the 1920 civilian war honours, was given a full naval funeral at Devonport Dockyard Church, attended by 400 officers and ratings.

SATURDAY 16th JANUARY 1932

Home Park witnessed the biggest win in Plymouth Argyle's history as the Pilgrims beat Millwall 8-1. Jack Vidler scored a hat-trick as Argyle scored six in the final half-hour of the Second Division game.

MONDAY 17th JANUARY 1898

The Plymouth-Yealmpton branch of the Great Western Railway was officially opened. The service, which ran from Plymouth Millbay and stopped at Billacombe, Brixton, Steer Point and Elburton Cross, closed in July 1930 but was re-opened during World War II to cater for Plymothians that had moved out of town following the air-raids on the city.

TUESDAY 18th JANUARY 1944

Prime Minister Winston Churchill made the final of his Second World War visits to Plymouth. He landed amidst great secrecy aboard the battleship HMS *King George V*, after talks with Allied leaders President Roosevelt, Premier Stalin and Generalissimo Chiang Kai Chek at Cairo and Teheran, to catch a train to London. His first visit to Plymouth was in 1940, when the First Lord of the Admiralty welcomed home the cruiser HMS *Exeter* after her victory against the *Graf Spee* in the Battle of the River Plate. When he returned in May 1941, it was in the wake of the Luftwaffe's springtime devastation of the city. The following year, he flew into Plymouth Sound after visiting America, and even had a stint at piloting his flying-boat on the 3,300-mile journey.

TUESDAY 19th JANUARY 2010

No less an organ than *The Times* of London reported sad news: "A cat that became famous for hitching a lift on buses in Devon has died after being hit by a car. Casper became a familiar sight in Plymouth, waiting at bus stops, being let on by drivers, then roaming the city. Last year, it emerged that he had been a regular on the No. 3 service for four years, with drivers knowing to let him off at his home stop at Barne Barton. The cat is thought to have been the victim of a hit-and-run. A notice posted at his stop reads: 'Many local people knew Casper who... enjoyed the bus journeys. He will be greatly missed'."

SUNDAY 20th JANUARY 1850

A public meeting regarding the imminent opening of a wash-house for the poor was held in Plymouth Guildhall. The wash-house was in Hoegate Street and its arrival followed the publication, three years earlier, of the findings of an inquiry into sanitary conditions in the city. Prompted by a cholera epidemic, the inquiry found more than 11,000 Plymothians lived in single rooms; cooking, sleeping and eating within the same four walls, often with other family members, as well as, crucially, washing and drying their clothes.

SUNDAY 21st JANUARY 1973

Royal Navy frigate HMS *Scylla* collided with the Torpoint Ferry in fog. The ferry's hull was split near the bows, leaving a three-foot-wide gash from handrail to waterline. No-one was injured, but her captain was court-martialled and found negligent. It was the start of an eventful career for the last Royal Navy frigate – to be built at Devonport – that included: mixing it with the Icelandic gunboat *Aegir* during the Cod Wars; taking part in the Queen's Silver Jubilee celebrations; bringing relief to the Cayman Islands after Hurricane Charley; and being part of the Armilla Patrol in the Middle East. In March 2004, following decommissioning, she was scuttled off Whitsand Bay to form a new artificial reef and diving location – the first-ever deliberate sinking of a redundant warship anywhere in Europe.

TUESDAY 22nd JANUARY 1867

Inventor Sir William Harris – 'Thunder-and-Lightning' Harris – died aged 84. Sir William came from an established family of Plymouth solicitors and qualified in medicine at university, so it was a surprise that he made his name as the inventor of a successful system of lightning conductors for ships. Certainly, the government were suspicious of the man honoured as a fellow of the Royal Society for his paper entitled *On the Relative Powers of Various Metallic Substances as Conductors of Electricity* as it took them nearly 30 years, and a great deal of persuasion by Harris and his backers, to introduce the new method to their vessels. His system, the hallmark of which was that the metal was permanently fixed in the masts and extended throughout the hull, was adopted in the Russian navy – and Harris honoured by the Tsar – before he succeeded in removing the prejudices against it in England.

THIS PLAQUE COMMEMORATES THE SAILING OF
THE SIX PLYMOUTH COMPANY VESSELS
CARRYING SETTLERS FROM CORNWALL, DEVON AND DORSET
TO ESTABLISH THE SETTLEMENT OF NEW PLYMOUTH
IN THE COLONY OF NEW ZEALAND.

WILLIAM BRYAN	BARQUE	312 TONS	SAILED 19 NOVEMBER 1840
AMELIA THOMPSON	BARQUE	477 TONS	SAILED 25 MARCH 1841
ORIENTAL	BARQUE	506 TONS	SAILED 2 JUNE 1841
TIMANDRA	BARQUE	382 TONS	SAILED 2 NOVEMBER 1841
BLENHEIM	BARQUE	374 TONS	SAILED 2 JULY 1842
ESSEX	BARQUE	329 TONS	SAILED 3 SEPTEMBER 1842

UNVEILED BY THE LORD MAYOR OF PLYMOUTH
COUNCILLOR GORDON DRAPER
AND HIS WORSHIP THE MAYOR OF NEW PLYMOUTH
D.L.LEAN. J.P. ESQ.
ON THIS 25TH DAY OF JULY 1988

THURSDAY 22nd JANUARY 1801

Vice-Admiral of the Blue Horatio Nelson was granted the freedom of the city of Plymouth.

TUESDAY 22nd JANUARY 1901

Plymouth was due to see the reopening of the Royal Eye Infirmary after it moved to Mutley, but the ceremony was postponed following the unforeseen death of Queen Victoria the previous day. The restaging of the reopening was presided over by Lady Mary Parker ten months later, Victoria's successor King Edward VII having seen fit to continue the Royal Patronage.

WEDNESDAY 23rd JANUARY 1918

Plymouth-born Sir Alexander Rendel died. There was never much doubt what career-path Sir Alexander would follow. The eldest son of city engineer James Rendel, whose brother George was also an engineer, followed in the family business after being educated at Trinity College, Cambridge, and was responsible for the Royal Albert Dock in London and the Albert and Edinburgh Docks in Leith. He married Eliza Hobson, daughter of Captain William Hobson, the first Governor of New Zealand, at the Parish Church of Stoke Damerel. The Reverend James Elliot, the uncle of the bride, officiated.

FRIDAY 24th JANUARY 1840

Henry Tufnell was elected Member of Parliament for Plymouth Devonport in a by-election and held the seat for 14 years. He held minor posts in the governments of Lord Melbourne and Lord John Russell and was made a Privy Councillor in 1850. Along with George Cornewall Lewis, he translated Otfried Müller's book *The History and Antiquities of the Doric Race* into English. You've read it, haven't you?

SATURDAY 25th JANUARY 1840

The Plymouth Company of New Zealand was founded. Eleven months later, they despatched the first party of 64 adults and 70 children to the land of the Long White Cloud aboard the *William Bryan*. The ship's captain, Alexander McLean, eventually put everyone down at Taranaki on North Island, where they moved their belongings to the site of their home from home – New Plymouth. The Plymouth Company sent out a total of six ships, carrying nearly 1,000 emigrants, before running out of funds.

MONDAY 25th JANUARY 1960

The body of Eva Booth was found in a cupboard at her home in Venn Way, Hartley. She had clearly been attacked although her assailant has never been found. The coroner did not think that her demise was deliberate, surmising that: "Perhaps her attacker hadn't meant to kill her, and hid her in the cupboard because he was panicking." The police held a contrary view, believing that the old lady got into an argument and was subsequently attacked and suffocated. The coroner's jury agreed and returned a verdict of murder by a person, or persons, unknown.

SATURDAY 26th JANUARY 1760

Sir George Pocock was elected Member of Parliament for Plymouth, the beginning of an eight-year term during which he effectively turned his back on his career in the Royal Navy. He was promoted to Rear Admiral in 1755, Vice-Admiral in 1756 and Admiral in 1761, at which time he also acquired his 'Sir'. He did not undertake further service following his marriage in 1763 and later asked to be retired from the Admiral's list, possibly in disgust at the appointment of Sir Charles Saunders, his junior, to be Lord of the Admiralty. However, the large fortune he had acquired and his nuptials – he married Sophia Pitt, the granddaughter of Sir Francis Drake – probably played a part in his decision.

TUESDAY 26th JANUARY 1796

Admiral Sir Edward Pellew had quite a naval pedigree, seeing service in the American War of Independence, the French Revolutionary War, and the Napoleonic War before eventually becoming commander-in-chief, Plymouth, from 1817 to 1821. However, for all his courage and leadership in battle, it was for peacetime bravery that Sir Edward merits a mention. In the first month of 1796, the East Indiaman *Dutton* was carrying troops bound for the West Indies when, in heavy seas caused by gale-force winds, it was wrecked in Plymouth Sound. Sir Edward swam out to the wreck and established a lifeline so that all but four people on board were saved. His heroism is recognised by Thomas Luny's painting *The Wreck of the East Indiaman 'Dutton' at Plymouth Sound, 26 January 1796*, which makes up for in style what it lacks in a pithy title and which can be seen at the National Maritime Museum, Greenwich.

TUESDAY 27th JANUARY 1254

Plymouth was upgraded from a small fishing village – known then as Sutton, from 'South Town' – to a market town by Royal Charter. At the time, Plymouth belonged to the Prior of Plympton, the head of an Augustinian order, who had been given it, along with other parts of the manor of Sutton, by the Valletort family. The practice was for the Prior to turn a village into a town by establishing a market, which would then attract merchants and craftsmen to live and work there. As the Prior of Plympton (a larger and older town than Sutton) held the market rights, there was some debate about who was Lord of the Manor. The judgment was that the original Sutton was owned by the Prior, land to the south was owned by John Valletort, and the port was the King's.

TUESDAY 27th JANUARY 1596

Sir Francis Drake died, aged 55, of 'the bloody flux' (probably dysentery), while his flagship, *Defiance*, was anchored off the coast of Portobelo, Panama. He was buried at sea in a lead coffin, and has been sought by divers ever since.

MONDAY 28th JANUARY 1788

'Australia's First Fleet' – the *Alexander*, the *Borrowdale*, the *Charlotte*. the *Fishburn*, the *Friendship*, the *Golden Grove*, the *Lady Penrhyn*, the *Prince of Wales*, the *Scarborough*, HMS *Sirius* and HMS *Supply*, containing more than 700 Westcountry convicts that had left England more than 10 months previously – arrived in a land Down Under at Port Jackson. Thus the first British colony in Australia was established in what later became Sydney, New South Wales, under Captain Arthur Phillip. Transport ships the *Charlotte* and the *Friendship* had left Plymouth in March 1787 as part of a fleet that comprised: more than 759 convicts (including 188 women); 700 merchant seamen, Royal Navy and Marine personnel and families; 209 fowls; 74 pigs; 35 ducks; 29 sheep; 29 geese; 19 goats; 18 turkeys; five cows; four stallions; three mares; two bulls; and quite probably Uncle Tom Cobley. The fleet had originally arrived at Botany Bay more than a week earlier but the area was deemed to be unsuitable for settlement because of a lack of fresh water, even though it had been recommended by Captain James Cook in 1770.

TUESDAY 29th JANUARY 1980

Commonwealth Games double-medallist athlete Katherine Endacott was born in Plymouth. Endacott originally finished out of the medals in the 100m individual final in Delhi 2010, but, five days later, found herself awarded the runner-up's silver. She had been bumped up to bronze after the disqualification, for a false start, of first-place finisher, Australian Sally Pearson. Then Nigeria's Damola Osayemi, who had been promoted into the gold medal position, failed a drugs test. Later in the Games, Endacott won gold – this time simply by finishing first – as part of an England women's 4 x 100m relay quartet which also included Montell Douglas, Laura Turner and Abi Oyepitan.

FRIDAY 30th JANUARY 2009

Nicky Reilly pleaded guilty to launching a failed nail-bomb suicide bid at the Giraffe restaurant in Exeter the previous May. Reilly was the only person injured when he accidentally set off his home-made bomb in a toilet of the restaurant. On the one hand, Reilly, 22, a Muslim convert from Stonehouse in Plymouth who appeared in court as Mohamad Abdulaziz Rashid Saeed, was obsessed with martyrdom and wanted to cause as much death and injury as possible. On the other, he suffered from Asperger's syndrome, had a mental age of 10, and was described by his lawyer as the "least cunning" person ever to have been charged with terrorism. He was jailed for a minimum of 18 years. After his conviction, counter-terrorism officials said that extremists had taken advantage of his low IQ to groom him.

WEDNESDAY 31st JANUARY 1940

HMS *Ajax* arrived back in Devonport Dockyard after its historic action against the German *Admiral Graf Spee* in the Battle of the River Plate, the first major naval confrontation of the Second World War. *Ajax* was the flagship of Commodore Henry Harwood's Force G and was hit seven times during the hunt for the German pocket battleship off the South American coast. However, she had her revenge on the *Graf Spee* during the Battle of the River Plate in December 1939. Earlier that year, *Ajax* had helped relief work after an earthquake in the Chilean city of Concepcion, action which later saw surviving members of HMS *Ajax* awarded medals from the Chilean government.

FEBRUARY

SATURDAY 1st FEBRUARY 1896

The fish market on the Barbican, built on reclaimed land, was opened. Congestion caused by the to-ing and fro-ing of emigration ships and the burgeoning fishing industry had necessitated widening the quay near the Mayflower Steps and this allowed the market to be established. It later moved to Sutton Harbour and was replaced by the Plymouth Barbican Glassworks, purveyors of the finest Dartington Crystal.

SATURDAY 1st FEBRUARY 1941

A Toc H hostel was opened in Plymouth's Union Street – a gift from the British War Relief Society of America, a non-military charity created in 1939 to provide welfare and support for soldiers in Europe which raised funds by selling souvenirs in America and Europe, and holding craft fairs and garden parties. Toc H came into being in Poperinge, Belgium, during World War I when the Reverend Philip 'Tubby' Clayton took over a large old house close to the Western Front and created a home-from-home for allied troops. The 'Old House' was christened 'Talbot House' (after Lt. Gilbert Talbot, who died at Ypres) and became known by its initials – in the Army Signallers' language of the day, Toc H. Thousands of men found peace and a sense of physical and spiritual re-creation in the house, and many of these came out of the war with a new or strengthened Christian faith. Toc H grew around the world as they worked to perpetuate the new fellowship they had found in the 'Old House'.

TUESDAY 2nd FEBRUARY 1790

Marine biologist William Leach was born in Plymouth, where he began his life's work by collecting marine samples from the Sound. At the age of 23, he became assistant librarian in the Zoological Department at the British Museum and set about sorting out the collections. He was made assistant keeper of the natural history department and became an expert on crustaceans and molluscs before being elected a fellow of the Royal Society. His system of naming his finds was esoteric – he called nine genera after Caroline, or anagrams of that name, leading to speculation that Caroline was his mistress. He resigned in 1822 after suffering a nervous breakdown due to overwork, not trying to find a tenth anagram of Caroline.

SUNDAY 3rd FEBRUARY 2002

Seven people were arrested at Devonport Dockyard during a protest over the refit of Trident ballistic missile-armed submarine HMS *Vanguard*. The seven – Sue Brackenbury, Richard Holt, Margaret Jones, Erica Wilson, Liz Wilson, Jill Wood and Angie Zelter – blocked the yard's Drake Gate before being removed and charged with obstructing the highway. *Vanguard*'s refit included the removal and replacement of the fuel rods that power its nuclear reactor and was completed in June 2004.

THURSDAY 4th FEBRUARY 1819

The original Athenaeum, home to the Plymouth Institution for the promotion of Science, Literature and the Liberal Arts, was formally opened by the Reverend Robert Lampen in Derry's Cross. Designed by John Foulston, an eccentric cove who had racked up in Plymouth after winning a competition to design the city's Royal Hotel, the Athenaeum is believed to be the first example of a true Grecian temple to be attempted in Britain. There was a frieze in the lecture room which was "cast from the famous Elgin collection... presented to the Institution in the most gracious and munificent manner by His Majesty King George IV". It was also said that the Apollo was the likeness of Admiral Sir Thomas Byam Martin, the Venus was that of inventor General Sir William Congreve, and the Antinous was that of the Earl of Morley, John Parker, second Baron Boringdon.

SATURDAY 4th FEBRUARY 1922

Jack Tripp, once described as 'the John Gielgud of pantomime dames', was born in Plymouth. Tripp was destined to tread the boards from a very early age, when he appeared in local clubs billed as 'Plymouth's Fred Astaire'. He served in the Royal Electrical and Mechanical Engineers during the Second World War before joining Stars in Battledress and performing in Europe and the Middle East. After the war, the smell of cordite and the roar of the guns were replaced by the smell of the greasepaint and roar of the crowd as Tripp took up acting, singing and dancing professionally. He appeared in at least 35 pantomimes as a dame, wearing ever more elaborate costumes. His last performance was in *Mother Goose* in Plymouth in 1996, the same year that he was made an MBE for his 'services to pantomime'. Oh yes he was.

THURSDAY 5th FEBRUARY 1874

Sir John Puleston was elected Conservative Member of Parliament for Devonport. A Welshman who emigrated to America, he became editor of the *Phoenixville Guardian* before moving on and leaving behind massive debts. He then invested in railroads, developed his political contacts, and became secretary to a Peace Commission that was set up prior to the American Civil War. His responsibilities included presenting reports to Abraham Lincoln. When war broke out, Puleston was appointed military agent for the state of Pennsylvania. After the war, he became a broker on Wall Street before returning to Blighty and winning Devonport. Five years after his election, he visited Philadelphia on official business and was reminded of his debts. He searched them all out and repaid them in full. He died a bankrupt. An honourable one, though.

THURSDAY 6th FEBRUARY 1595

Sir Walter Raleigh left England to sail to the New World to search for the city of El Dorado, not so much for personal gain, more to get back in Queen Elizabeth I's good books. Three years earlier, Elizabeth had discovered Sir Walter's secret marriage to one of her maids of honour, Elizabeth Throckmorton, and, by way of a wedding present, had sent the happy couple on a less than romantic break in the Tower of London. On his release, in an attempt to please Her Jealous Majesty, Sir Walter set off to find the fabled 'Golden Land' rumoured to be situated in what is now Venezuela. Not surprisingly, he did not find it.

SATURDAY 7th FEBRUARY 1959

The curtain came down on the New Palace Theatre of Varieties on Union Street during the pantomime *Little Miss Muffet*. It reopened in 1962 with another panto, *Sinbad the Sailor*, but closed three years later after being bought by a Manchester club-owner in order to present bingo, wrestling and striptease. Not at the same time, although that would have been interesting. It was later sold to EMI and re-opened again as a theatre in April 1977 with the English Music Theatre Company's *Magic Flute*. After three years, it ceased trading again. The Grade II listed building did re-open once more, in May 1981 with Danny La Rue in revue, but finally closed in 1983 and became The Academy nightclub.

SATURDAY 8th FEBRUARY 1997

Plymouth-based newspaper the *Western Morning News* was transformed to tabloid size after 137 years as a broadsheet. Editor Colin Davidson was so keen not to be tarnished by association with the worst excesses of the national tabloids that the resized product was always referred to as 'compact', rather than 'tabloid'.

FRIDAY 9th FEBRUARY 1979

Trevor Francis, the most famous Plymouth footballer never to play football for Plymouth, became England's first £1m player when Brian Clough bought him for Nottingham Forest from Birmingham City. With typical eccentricity and an eye for a headline, Cloughie insisted the fee was actually £999,999, although the papers got their headlines when they added in the tax. It proved money well spent as Trevor led Forest to two successive European Cup triumphs, scoring the winner in the first against Malmo in 1979. He also won 52 caps for England, scoring 11 goals, and played for Sampdoria, in Italy, Manchester City, Rangers and Queens Park Rangers. He was, according to England manager Fabio Capello, the best English player to have ever played in Italy's Serie A. As a striker, his success was due to split-second recognition of opportunity, great acceleration, and confidence in his own ability. Trevor had joined Birmingham City as a schoolboy, debuting in 1970, aged just 16, and made 278 League appearances, scoring 119 goals, before Forest came calling.

MONDAY 10th FEBRUARY 1879

Construction began of the Royal Naval Engineering College alongside the Dockyard wall at Keyham. The designer is thought to be Sir Charles Barry, the architect of the Houses of Parliament. The college provided all the engineering training previously given in the four Royal Dockyard Schools at Woolwich, Sheerness, Portsmouth and Devonport, as well as accommodation for all the Navy's engineer students. The subsequent need to expand away from the crowded Keyham site was achieved by the purchase of the Manadon estate in 1937, and nine years later, the whole of the RNEC complex was commissioned as HMS Thunderer. The Keyham building was used by the Devonport Dockyard Technical College before being demolished in 1985, with training being consolidated at RNEC Manadon, which itself closed in 1995. Engineer officers have since been trained at civilian universities and at the Navy's specialist establishments in Portsmouth.

MONDAY 11th FEBRUARY 1952

Work started on demolishing 'Tin Pan Alley' that had grown up after the Second World War in Drake Street. The occupants of Tin Pan Alley were previously traders from the pannier market who had been obliged to forfeit their place in favour of bombed-out chain stores such as Woolworth's and Marks & Spencer. Major retailers were given stalls in the pannier market building, while smaller ex-market traders opened for business in a line of temporary corrugated-iron stalls in the adjoining street.

SATURDAY 12th FEBRUARY 1944

The Manadon Field Hospital, at Manadon Vale, was opened after being built by the United States Construction Battalion from Quonset huts and stones, bricks and rubble left behind after the German air-raids on the city. The 500-bed capacity hospital was constructed in preparation for the D-Day landings in less than 10 weeks.

MONDAY 13th FEBRUARY 1804

The great Shakespearean actor-manager Samuel Phelps was born in Plymouth Dock. Phelps made his debut as Shylock in *The Merchant of Venice* at London's Haymarket Theatre in 1837 and later took over management of the then unfashionable Sadler's Wells Theatre and revolutionised the production of Shakespeare's plays by restoring them to the original text of the first folio for the first time since the Restoration. Phelps' most frequently performed role was Hamlet, but he also played Macbeth, Leontes, and Bottom and was generally considered the finest King Lear of his generation. Better, I suppose, than being generally considered the finest Bottom of his generation.

THURSDAY 14th FEBRUARY 1884

The statue of Sir Francis Drake, on Plymouth Hoe, overlooking Plymouth Sound, was unveiled by Lady Fuller Drake, a representative of the female line of Drake's brother, Thomas. The statue, with Drake holding a globe and sword, is a replica of one in Tavistock designed by Sir Joseph Boehm. The statue on the Hoe stands near to the place where, legend has it, Drake decided that he had time to finish his game of bowls before putting to sea to fight the Spanish Armada. Legend also reminds us that the decision was an easy one as the tide was out.

TUESDAY 15th FEBRUARY 1949

The Bank of England closed its branch in Bank of England Place, Plymouth, after more than 100 years of business. In January 1834, the Treasurer of the Navy requested that new branches be opened in Portsmouth, Plymouth, Chatham and Pembroke to facilitate the supply of money to the dockyards. The Bank agreed to open a branch in Plymouth, which took over the business of the loss-making Exeter branch. It opened on May 1st 1834 in a house in St Andrew's Terrace, with Robert Morris appointed agent. He continued until 1867, when he retired at the age of 80, having overseen a move to George Street in 1844. There was a gradual decline in the bank's usefulness, and Second World War damage led to its closure in 1949. Though only as a bank, public amenity – it later reopened as the Bank public house.

FRIDAY 16th FEBRUARY 1940

The ship's companies of HMS *Ajax* and *Exeter* marched through Plymouth to the Guildhall for a civic reception in honour of their part in the Battle of the River Plate. Exeter was laid down at Devonport in August 1928. At the outbreak of the Second World War, alongside cruisers *Ajax* and *Achilles*, she engaged the *Admiral Graf Spee* in the Battle of the River Plate, which culminated in the scuttling of the German battleship. *Exeter* operated as one division, and *Achilles* and *Ajax* the other, to split the enemy fire. *Exeter* was hit by seven 11-inch shells, and 61 crew were killed.

TUESDAY 17th FEBRUARY 1925

Ron Goodwin, one of Britain's foremost film composers, was born, in Swilly. Goodwin wrote the scores for more than 60 movies, including *Those Magnificent Men in Their Flying Machines* (They Go Up, Tiddly, Up, Up), but it was for war epics like *Where Eagles Dare*, *Battle of Britain* and *633 Squadron* that he is best remembered. He was also a major recording artist, and he and his concert orchestra were signed by the Beatles' producer George Martin. He was awarded a gold disc in 1975 for selling more than a million albums. Goodwin returned to his birthplace in 1980, when he was commissioned to write what became his *Drake 400 Suite* to commemorate the anniversary of Sir Francis's return to Plymouth.

MONDAY 17th FEBRUARY 1913

England defeated Wales 40-16 in a rugby league – or 'Northern Union', as it was then known – international in front of 7,000 spectators at South Devon Place, previously the home of Plymouth Rugby Football Club.

WEDNESDAY 18th FEBRUARY 2009

The biggest Royal Navy Task Force to deploy to the Far East in more than a decade set sail from Plymouth. HMS *Bulwark* led the Taurus deployment, which had been 18 months in the planning, comprising 12 ships, including a US Navy destroyer and a French Navy frigate. The Task Force conducted a wide range of activities – including maritime security operations and amphibious and anti-submarine warfare exercises – with 17 nations. At its height, 3,300 personnel took part in the 20,400-mile round-trip deployment.

TUESDAY 19th FEBRUARY 1935

Thomas Edward Shaw retired from the Royal Air Force, having been stationed at RAF Mount Batten for six years. Shaw was involved in the development of high-speed boats that later played an important role in rescuing airmen from the English Channel during the Battle of Britain but it is not for this that he achieved fame. He had legally changed his name to 'Shaw' in 1927, five years after joining the RAF, having been christened Thomas Edward Lawrence, aka 'Lawrence of Arabia'. Two months after leaving the service, he died in a motorcycle accident near his Dorset home. A plaque at Mount Batten reads: "Lawrence of Arabia 1888-1935. On his return from India in 1929, TE Lawrence, under the assumed name of Shaw, was posted to a flying-boat squadron at RAF Mount Batten. He remained in the marine craft section until his discharge." Nearby streets 'Lawrence Road' and 'Shaw Way' have been named in his honour.

WEDNESDAY 20th FEBRUARY 1884

Sergeant Francis Attwood, hero of the 1879 Anglo-Zulu War, died at home in Cremyll Street, aged 38. Attwood was awarded the Distinguished Conduct Medal for his actions at Rorke's Drift, and was buried with full military honours in Milehouse Cemetery. His headstone was damaged in World War II and, after Milehouse Cemetery was closed in 1967 and he was re-interred at Efford Cemetery, a new plaque in his honour was unveiled in 2009.

FRIDAY 21st FEBRUARY 1936

True Blue redhead Janet Fookes, Conservative Member of Parliament for Plymouth Drake for 23 years, was born. A former teacher, she entered into her long relationship with Plymouth in 1974, having been obliged to seek a new seat when her previous constituency of Merton and Morden was abolished. The revived Drake was far from a safe seat, as Fookes' majority of just 34 in her initial victory in 1974 showed, but she was destined to be its only MP until it, too, was abolished in 1997, seeing off many strong challenges. Such longevity has its political rewards: she was made a Dame Commander of the Order of the British Empire in 1989, was a Deputy Speaker of the House of Commons from 1992 until the 1997 General Election, and was made a Life Peer – Baroness Fookes, of Plymouth in the County of Devon – on retiring from the Commons.

MONDAY 21st FEBRUARY 2011

Financially struggling Plymouth Argyle were docked ten points by the Football League after announcing that the club intended to appoint an administrator as they battled to avoid liquidation. The punishment put the Pilgrims to the bottom of npower League One, ten points from safety, and contributed to their eventual relegation to the fourth tier of English football. Deputy chairman Paul Stapleton said: "This action gives the club protection from insolvency action from creditors."

WEDNESDAY 22nd FEBRUARY 1854

The American-built British ship *Parsee* departed Plymouth for a 102-day journey to Melbourne, Australia. She carried 493 emigrants, including 105 married couples, who landed near the mouth of the Brisbane River to start a new life. Many travelled as part of the Assisted British Immigrants Act which was active between 1839 and 1871. The assistance received by immigrants who were registered under this act was subsidised passage from Queen Victoria's government. Their journey was not uneventful. According to the *Sydney Morning Herald*: "Some of the seamen of this ship have behaved very badly. The second officer was placed in irons about three weeks ago, for threatening the captain's life, and eight of the seamen absconded from the ship on Tuesday last, in a boat... which had come alongside for a supply of fresh water."

WEDNESDAY 23rd FEBRUARY 1842

Cora Pearl, part of the demimonde, the 'half-world' between respectability and prostitution inhabited by the luxury courtesans of 19th-century Paris, was born Emma Elizabeth Crouch in Caroline Place, East Stonehouse, one of 16 children. Despite poor manners and incomprehensible French, she became the queen of Paris courtesans after moving to France as the mistress of London dancehall owner Robert Bignall. When Robert returned to England and his family, Emma stayed behind, taking the name 'Cora Pearl' just because she fancied the way that it sounded. Even those who found Cora Pearl vulgar admitted that her body was second to none, while her bosom was described as "marvellous and worthy of being moulded by some illustrious artist of antiquity". More importantly, Cora Pearl knew the art of displaying her beautiful body to full effect.

MONDAY 23rd FEBRUARY 1880

Isaac Foot, the founder of the Foot political dynasty, was born in Plymouth. Educated at Plymouth Public School and the Hoe Grammar School, he qualified as a solicitor in 1902 and set up the law firm 'Foot and Bowden' with his friend Edgar Bowden, which still existed as 'Foot-Anstey' more than 100 years later. Indefatigable Isaac served on Plymouth City Council for 20 years from 1907, becoming Deputy Mayor in 1920, when he represented Plymouth in the United States for the celebrations of the *Mayflower*'s tercentenary. After two unsuccessful attempts to win the Bodmin Parliamentary seat for the Liberals and being beaten by Nancy Astor in the Plymouth Sutton by-election of 1919, he finally took Bodmin at a 1922 by-election, retained it in the General Elections of 1922 and 1923, lost it in October 1924, and regained it in the 1929 General Election, when the Liberals took all five Cornish seats, this time holding it for six years. In 1931, he became Minister of Mines in the National Government, but resigned in protest at the protectionist Ottawa Trade Agreements. He fought two more elections, at St. Ives in 1937, and Tavistock in 1945, losing both. Following his final defeat, he was chosen unanimously as Lord Mayor of Plymouth, despite not being a member of the council, and, two years later, became President of the Liberal Party. He was far from inactive in retirement. He owned a library of more than 70,000 books at his home near Callington and would wake at 5am in order to read them. He also taught himself Greek to be able to read the New Testament in the original.

SUNDAY 24th FEBRUARY 1833

Thomas Tyrwhitt, Member of Parliament for Plymouth between 1806 and 1812, died aged 70. A private secretary to the Prince of Wales, he created a small village on Dartmoor which he named 'Prince's Town', in honour of his former employer. He intended to turn the desolate moor into a thriving place to live and work and persuaded the government to erect a gaol to house prisoners of the Napoleonic Wars. Realising that his beloved Prince's Town lacked good communication with Plymouth, he proposed to the Plymouth Chamber of Commerce that a railway between the two would be an excellent idea, and, on 12th August 1819, Sir Thomas laid the first rail of a line that eventually opened in September 1823.

SATURDAY 25th FEBRUARY 1984

A crowd of 10,023 attended Home Park to see Plymouth Argyle beat Hull 2-0 in a Third Division game. At least, that is what the record books say. However, the figure was probably boosted by some people paying at the gate twice to ensure that they had enough vouchers to claim a ticket for the forthcoming FA Cup quarter-final against Derby County.

THURSDAY 26th FEBRUARY 1959

Motor entrepreneur William Mumford, the Richard Branson of his day, died, aged 80. William started his own coach-building business in Glanville Street in 1900, aged just 21. Three years later, he moved the burgeoning business to Ebrington Street, where he built Plymouth's first taxi and from where he launched the city's first bus service, between Plymouth and Crownhill. He failed to complete a transport hat-trick when plans to build a plane were abandoned for want of an appropriate engine. Mumford Ltd continued to expand, moving to Billacombe, before William retired in 1930, leaving the business to his four sons. His family kept the Mumford name alive and synonymous with motoring in Plymouth into the 21st century and a fourth generation.

SATURDAY 27th FEBRUARY 1904

Devonport Park's Doris Gun Memorial was unveiled by Admiral Sir Edward Seymour, commander-in-chief at Devonport, and Vice-Admiral Sir Robert Harris. The memorial is dedicated to the men from HMS *Doris* who lost their lives in the Boer war, during which the pom-pom gun was claimed as a prize by the ship's crew who had assisted in the taking of Paardeberg.

THURSDAY 28th FEBRUARY 1974

"The most politically incorrect, outspoken, iconoclastic and reckless politician of our times" was elected Member of Parliament for Plymouth Sutton. Conservative Alan Clark, who was given that epithet by former Chancellor of the Exchequer Norman Lamont, represented the ward for 18 years, during which time he served his nation as Minister of Trade and Minister for Defence Procurement. He also earned the unique distinction of being the only MP ever to be accused of being drunk at the Dispatch Box in the House of Commons. He later admitted that his befuddlement at the complexities of equal pay regulations in the House had not been helped by a preceding 'wine-tasting dinner'.

SUNDAY 28th FEBRUARY 2010

Radio Plymouth went on air for the first time at 10am. TV personality, ex-Plymouth Hospital radio presenter and former BBC broom-cupboard resident Philip Schofield was an investor in the station, along with several other individuals and the Sunrise Radio Group.

WEDNESDAY 29th FEBRUARY 1928

Edward Dingle, the founder of Messrs E Dingle & Company, was buried at the Plymouth Old Cemetery – later Ford Park Cemetery – having died four days previously at the age of 87. Forty-three years later, the business he had started as a drapery shop at 30 Bedford Street in 1880 was bought by the House of Fraser for just over £6m. The current building was designed by Thomas Tait and was one of the earliest post-war constructions in Plymouth. It was also the first major post-war department store to open in Britain, the first in the South West to be fitted with escalators, and the first building in Plymouth to mark the boundaries of Armada Way, Royal Parade and New George Street. A little known fact about Dingles is that there is an Edwardian management suite that was removed from a house during the Second World War blitz, put into storage, and placed in the rebuilt store.

MARCH

WEDNESDAY 1st MARCH 1826/TUESDAY 1st MARCH 1910

It may have amused George Bignell, had he known it, that he died on his 84th birthday for, among his many roles in life he was Registrar of Births and Deaths for Stonehouse. That followed his first career, in the Royal Marines, who he served aboard HMS *Superb*, one of the Navy's last all-wooden ships. During his 22-year service, he developed a passion for insects and his later work with ichneumonidae (parasitic wasps to you and me) was without peer. He discovered 19 new species, two of which are named after him. He was a member of the Plymouth Institution – becoming President – and a Fellow of the Royal Entomological Society of London. A large collection of his specimens can be seen at Plymouth Museum and some are housed at London's Natural History Museum.

THURSDAY 2nd MARCH 1939

Mutley Railway Station, the 'Station of the Gentry', was closed. Plymouth's second permanent station – after Millbay – had been opened by the South Devon Railway on 1st August 1871. Within five years, it became a joint station used also by the London and South Western Railway trains from Tavistock. Located near Ermington Terrace and Napier Terrace, it was closed when track alterations saw North Road station take over as the city's main station.

TUESDAY 3rd MARCH 1942

Six World War II heroes of the City of Plymouth Police, and firefighters, attended Buckingham Palace to be presented with the British Empire Medal for bravery and gallant conduct during the Luftwaffe raids of 1941. Inspector Herbert Beswick, William Edgecombe, PC Robert Eakers, former PC Alan Hill, Arthur Larson, and Private Leslie Stephens received their awards from King George VI.

WEDNESDAY 3rd MARCH 2010

Michael Mackintosh Foot, Green Army 1921 to 2010; MP for Plymouth Devonport 1945 to 1955; Leader of Her Majesty's Opposition from 1980 to 1983; Plymouth Argyle director 2001 to 2005; editor of *Tribune* and the *Evening Standard*; biographer of Jonathan Swift and Aneurin Bevan; and passionate supporter of the Campaign for Nuclear Disarmament, British withdrawal from the European Economic Community, and the Pilgrims, died. He had been born in Lipson Terrace, Plymouth, nearly 97 years earlier.

SUNDAY 4th MARCH 2007

Plymouth Raiders upset Newcastle Eagles and the odds to win the British Basketball League Trophy. Raiders reached their first Trophy final by finishing first in a group also containing Guildford, Reading and Worthing and then crushing Leicester 83-64 in the semi-finals. Not only were their opponents in the final a side that had beaten Raiders by 24 points in a league encounter a few weeks earlier, but also the match was being played on the Eagles' home turf of Newcastle's Metro Radio Arena. Astonishingly, Raiders hung tough to come away with a 74-65 victory.

THURSDAY 5th MARCH 1668

Baptist minister Abraham Cheare died following three years' incarceration on St Nicholas' Island, now more commonly known as 'Drake's Island'. Cheare had been a victim of the Act of Uniformity in 1662, a legacy of the English Civil War during which the Puritans had abolished many features of the Church of England. The Act proscribed the form of public prayers, administration of sacraments, and other rites of the Established Church. 'Dissenters', like Calvinist Baptist Cheare were subjected to persecution, and he spent more than three years in Exeter jail before being released in 1665. He had barely returned to his work when his enemies obtained an order for his perpetual banishment to St Nicholas' Island, which had been converted into a state prison in 1643, where he died.

MONDAY 6th MARCH 1598

After a couple of false starts, the Earl of Cumberland, George Clifford, set sail from Plymouth on the *Scourge of Malice*, the flagship of a fleet of 20 vessels, under orders from Queen Elizabeth I to capture Brazil from the Spanish. They made it to San Juan, in what is now Puerto Rico, but was then a Spanish stronghold protected by a network of fortifications to protect the transport of gold and silver from the New World to Europe. Clifford landed troops and laid siege to the city but was forced to abandon it after 65 days when he lost 400 troops to an epidemic of dysentery, double the number that were killed in the skirmishes. Before they left, they sacked the town, burning houses to the ground and laying claim to, among other things, the cathedral bells and 2,000 slaves.

TUESDAY 7th MARCH 1911

Film director Jill Craigie was born. Craigie was the wife of Michael Foot, whom she met in Plymouth during the making of her film *The Way We Live*. After visiting the city, she discovered that many Plymothians were confused by the 'Plan for Plymouth', the designs of James Paton Watson and Sir Patrick Abercrombie to rebuild the city after World War II. She decided to make a film that clarified the planning issues and provided a platform for the townspeople, particularly women, to voice their ideas about housing. J Arthur Rank financed the film, which is told through the eyes of a bombed-out family. Craigie did not want to impose her own opinions on the film – she saw herself as "an interpreter of the ideas of the architects, the town councillors and the people of Plymouth", as is evident in the procession sequence which closes the film, for which Craigie persuaded 3,000 people to take part. In Plymouth, the film broke all box-office records and, as one local observer put it; "revived the interest of the man in the street in what is to be done to erase the scar which lies across our city."

MONDAY 8th MARCH 2010

'The Reel Plymouth', previously the ABC cinema in Derry's Cross, played host to life-sized white rabbits, playing cards and mad hatters as the city staged its own premiere of Disney film *Alice in Wonderland*. The audience comprised many of the 250 extras that appeared in Tim Burton's multi-million-pound movie which had been shot in part at Antony House, near Torpoint, some 18 months earlier. Other scenes had been shot on Plymouth's Barbican but did not make it into the movie.

MONDAY 9th MARCH 1891

'The Blizzard of the West' started, effectively cutting off much of Cornwall and Devon from the rest of Britain for four days. On the first night, a Yelverton-Princetown train was trapped in a snowdrift, leaving its three crew and six passengers huddled for warmth in a carriage overnight before being rescued by a local farmer tending to his sheep. HMS *Lion* and HMS *Implacable* were grounded off Plymouth, 14 other ships sunk, and approximately 220 deaths were attributed to the weather conditions.

THE BARBICAN. NO WHITE RABBITS PLAYING CARDS, OR MAD HATTERS, HERE

SATURDAY 9th MARCH 1833

William Groom, British convict and Australian politician was born in Plymouth. Groom was educated at St Andrew's College and apprenticed to a baker before being transported to Australia for seven years after being convicted of embezzlement at the age of 13. Down Under, he was released, convicted of a similar offence, released again and then became a pillar of Queensland society. He was owner of *The Chronicle* (Toowoomba) newspaper, one of the founders of the Toowoomba Permanent Building Society, involved in the creation of the Toowoomba Racecourse, the School of Arts and many other establishments. He was Toowoomba's inaugural mayor, a position he filled three times, and elected representative in the Queensland Colonial Government before, in 1901, becoming the only transported convict to ever sit as a member of the Australian Parliament. However, the reformed embezzler was also the first serving member of the Australian Parliament to die. Having climbed to the top of the greasy pole, he passed away at the first Commonwealth Parliament meeting in Melbourne as a result of a combination of bronchial catarrh and heart failure. He was succeeded in Parliament by his third son, Littleton Groom, who won Australia's first federal by-election and later became Speaker of the House of Representatives.

MONDAY 10th MARCH 1941

The Duke of Kent arrived in Plymouth for a four-day visit. A frequent visitor to the city, Prince George was killed the following year. He is the only member of the Royal family in modern times to have died on active service, crashing on Eagle's Mount Rock, near Dunbeath, in Caithness, on his way to Iceland to meet senior members of the US military.

SUNDAY 11th MARCH 2007

Plymouth Argyle manager Ian Holloway could not hide his bitter disappointment after the Pilgrims slipped out of the FA Cup, losing a gripping Home Park quarter-final clash with Watford 1-0. Algerian Hameur Bouazza scored the only goal of the game but there was no doubt who Watford's hero was – England international goalkeeper Ben Foster. "I don't like him at all because he has ruined my dream," said Holloway. "He has made some great saves, which is what he is paid to do. He has cracked my heart."

THURSDAY 12th MARCH 2009

Kate Nesbitt, a Royal Navy medic from Plymouth, was the first female member of the Senior Service – and only the second woman in the British Armed Forces – to be awarded the Military Cross. On this day in Afghanistan, Nesbitt administered emergency medical treatment to Lance Corporal John List while under ambush fire from Taliban forces. List, a 22-year-old soldier of 1st Battalion, The Rifles, was shot in the neck, the bullet going through his top lip, rupturing his jaw, and exiting his neck. Nesbitt ran 70 metres under fire and administered first aid, stemming the blood loss and providing List with another airway, for 45 minutes, during which time they both were subject to gun and rocket fire from the Taliban forces. Nesbitt was presented with her Military Cross by Prince Charles at Buckingham Palace. The citation read: "Nesbitt's actions throughout a series of offensive operations were exemplary; under fire and under pressure, her commitment and courage were inspirational and made the difference between life and death. She performed in the highest traditions of her service."

TUESDAY 13th MARCH 1787

Transport ships the *Friendship* and the *Charlotte* were loaded with convicts at Plymouth before joining nine other ships of the First Fleet at Portsmouth to set sail for Australia to establish the first European colony. *Friendship* arrived at Botany Bay on January 19, 1788, and *Charlotte* a day later.

WEDNESDAY 14th MARCH 1923

The Devonport War Memorial was unveiled by Field Marshal the Right Honourable the Lord Methuen. A Cornish granite Gothic Cross, 33 feet high and capped with an ornamental lantern and cross, it contains the figure of Victory in white marble and a bronze of the Borough arms. The reverse contains a bronze panel with the inscription "To the immortal memory of the citizens of Devonport who fell in the Great War" alongside the insignia of the Royal Navy, the Army and the Royal Air Force.

TUESDAY 15th MARCH 1887

Two bullocks waiting to be transported by ferry from Torpoint to Devonport for slaughter took fright and played havoc with disembarking passengers, killing a wine and spirit merchant from Devonport.

TUESDAY 16th MARCH 1852

The foundation-stone of the Plymouth Workhouse was laid. Nearly 150 years later, after being enlarged several times, it closed. In between times, it had been renamed Greenbank Infirmary in 1909, and, after the workhouse system disappeared it became the Plymouth City Hospital. To thousands of Plymothians who were born, worked or died there, though, it was known simply as 'Freedom Fields'.

SUNDAY 17th MARCH 1940

Cinemas in Plymouth opened for the first time on a Sunday.

MONDAY 17th MARCH 1947

At 8.15am, in Raleigh Street, Plymouth, corporation workmen started work on the reconstruction of the city centre following the Second World War blitz, when they began excavation work to place a sewer. The moment is commemorated in an engraved kerbstone in the current Derry's Cross roundabout and is atop a box containing an aerial photograph of Royal Parade and council papers. On the same day, St Andrew's Church held a service "to afford an opportunity to the Council to dedicate itself to the task of the re-building of the City".

SUNDAY 18th MARCH 1838

James Loveless, James Brine, and Thomas and John Stanfield – four of the Tolpuddle Martyrs – returned to Britain from exile in Australia, landing at Plymouth's Sutton Harbour after being pardoned following a great deal of public protest and a lengthy legal battle. Four years earlier, they were among six farmers from Dorset convicted for daring to form a trade union and were deported Down Under. A plaque placed on the Barbican by members of trades unions affiliated to the Plymouth and District Trades Council commemorates the landing – "Freedom and Justice was their Cause".

FRIDAY 19th MARCH 2010

Tolls on the Tamar Bridge and Torpoint Ferry were increased by 50% – the first increase in cash tolls for nearly 16 years, and the first increase in pre-paid tolls for 13 years. The cost to take a car from Cornwall into Plymouth rose from £1 to £1.50 and pre-paid tolls rose to 75p per crossing.

THURSDAY 20th MARCH 1941

'The Plymouth Blitz' – a devastating and ruinous assault on the city in three waves – began at 8.39pm. Heinkel III bombers started the attack with a load of bombs that included 34 delayed-action high-explosive devices. They reached Plymouth before their pathfinders, who dropped their flares anyway. These were followed by 12,500 incendiaries and other high-explosive bombs. Within two hours of the attack, the Plymouth Fire Service had been supplemented by additional pumps from Barnstaple, Bodmin, Bridgwater, Exeter, Fowey, Kingsbridge, Launceston, Liskeard, Looe, Lostwithiel, Plympton, Saltash, Tavistock, Torpoint, Torquay, Wadebridge, Yelverton and Yeovil, as well as 21 pumps from naval and military establishments. The Plymouth City Hospital Maternity Ward received a direct hit, killing four nurses, three of them teenagers, and 19 children whose ages ranged from three years to just one week, the youngest being Harold Santilla, who died with his mother Dorothy, 24. It was not until the following morning that the fires were brought under control. Nearly 800 firemen, using more than 150 appliances, were then on duty. A few hours before the bombing began King George VI and Queen Elizabeth had been visiting the Royal Marine Barracks, the Royal Naval Barracks, the Royal Dockyard, and the Royal Naval Hospital.

FRIDAY 21st MARCH 1941

Almost to the hour, 24 hours later, the Nazis resumed their pummelling of Plymouth. Only two city centre buildings survived intact – the National Westminster Bank, in Bedford Street, and the offices of the Western Morning News Company, in Frankfort Street, both of which were spared a direct hit. St Andrew's Parish Church, the Guildhall, and the Municipal Offices were gutted, while the Plymouth Co-operative Society emporium was destroyed. Nearly 300 civilians were killed. The Devonport dockyards were, of course, the main target of the German bombers throughout the war but civilian casualties were very high and the dockyards continued to operate. In the 59 bombing attacks on Plymouth during the war, 1,172 civilians were killed and 4,448 injured. The resident population fell from 220,000 at the outbreak of war to, at one point, only 127,000, largely because of evacuations.

WEDNESDAY 21st MARCH 1962

On the 21st anniversary of the destruction of the old Municipal Offices, the new fully furnished Council House and Municipal Offices were officially handed over to Plymouth Corporation.

SUNDAY 22nd MARCH 2009

The Merchant Navy and Royal Naval Reserves were awarded the Freedom of the City. Special scrolls were presented to representatives from the two organisations, before recruits paraded through the city centre. The Freedom of the City is the greatest ceremonial honour a local authority can bestow and gives martial organisations the privilege of marching into the city "with drums beating, colours flying, and bayonets fixed". The honour was granted in recognition of the organisations' long association with Plymouth and a mark of respect for "their critical and strategic roles, particularly in times of war and conflict".

MONDAY 23rd MARCH 1908

Mechanic turned surrealist artist Cecil Collins was born in Plymouth. A Devonport-based machine-worker, Cecil attended Plymouth School of Art from 1924 to 1927. From there, he gained a scholarship to the Royal College of Art, where he won the William Rothenstein Life Drawing Prize and went on to be widely regarded as England's most important visionary artist since William Blake.

MONDAY 23rd MARCH 2009

After nearly three and a half decades, Plymouth Sound radio station ceased to exist when it was renamed Heart FM as part of a national rebranding exercise by owners Global Radio. By this time, most of the station's programming was produced in London.

SATURDAY 24th MARCH 1832

William IV gave his Royal Assent to the Saltash Floating Bridge Act, which gave rights to the Earl of Morley and Sir William Molesworth, amongst others, to establish a steam-powered floating bridge, running along chains, across the Tamar.

WEDNESDAY 25th MARCH 1857

The Cathedral Church of Saint Mary and Saint Boniface, in Wyndham Street West, was opened with a Mass. The architects were Joseph and Charles Hansom. Joseph also registered the design of the Hansom safety cab and founded trade journal *The Builder*. The local men from Stonehouse who built his design were not fazed by the Royal Navy officer who fired new Turkish man-of-war guns in Plymouth Sound, causing subsidence. The Cathedral was consecrated by Bishop Vaughan in 1880.

FRIDAY 26th MARCH 1954

James Peters, the first black man to play rugby union for England, died. 'Darkie' Peters, as he was somewhat politically incorrectly known, was orphaned as a youngster after his Jamaican father had been mauled to death by lions in a training cage. As a young man, James moved to Plymouth from London and played rugby union for the town and for Devon. In 1906, he played for the county against the South Africans in front of 20,000 fans at the Plymouth County ground. However, he nearly did not. The tourists had belatedly noticed Peters' colour (presumably, they thought 'Darkie' referred to the colour of his hair) and initially refused to play. However, the South African High Commissioner feared a riot if the game was cancelled and persuaded the team to take the field. Peters, though, was shamefully withdrawn from the England squad later that year following similar complaints from the Springboks, who then played an all-white England. The following year, Peters played for England against Scotland. *The Sportsman* commented that the "dusky Plymouth man did many good things, especially in passing" while the *Yorkshire Post* pointed out, "his selection is by no means popular on racial grounds". James played one more international, against France, and scored a try. However, he was not picked for the next game against South Africa, again on racial grounds, and was never selected for England again. In 1910, Peters lost three fingers in a dockyard accident, but continued to play for Plymouth until 1912, when clubs in the South West of England attempted to join the Northern Union (later the Rugby League) and form a Western League of the Northern Union. Peters and his Plymouth team-mates were suspended for accepting payments, which was illegal according to the codes of rugby union, and Plymouth RFC were suspended by the Rugby Football Union, signalling the end of the club. Peters returned to his native north-west and played rugby league for Barrow and St Helens until his retirement.

FRIDAY 27th MARCH 1936

Plymouth's first milk bar was opened in Basket Street. The first pint of milk was drunk by Lady Astor. I bet she did not get the round in.

WEDNESDAY 28th MARCH 1877

The "dullest of stations", Plymouth North Road, was opened as a joint station for the Great Western Railway and the London and South Western Railway. It was expanded in 1908, but a major rebuilding scheme that started in 1938 was delayed by World War II and was not completed until 1962. John Betjeman was among those who did not pop a champagne cork on completion of the largest of the six surviving railway stations in the city. In his introduction to the *Book of the Great Western*, he wrote: "Plymouth (North Road), dullest of stations and no less dull now it has been rebuilt in copybook contemporary. The general grey slate and back gardens of Plymouth, as seen from the Great Western made the surprise of Saltash Bridge all the more exciting." It might be dull, but there is scarcely time for a dull moment at the station – it has the largest number of passengers starting and finishing their journeys of any in Devon.

MONDAY 29th MARCH 1585

Royal Assent was received by the Water Bill, meaning Plymouth's water supply could be derived from the River Meavy, on Dartmoor. Construction of the Plymouth Leat began four years later.

SATURDAY 30th MARCH 1861

Private Robert Hackett was hanged outside Exeter Prison. Robert could not hack it when he was on the receiving end of what he regarded an offensive remark by Sergeant Henry Jones at Millbay Barracks. "Only the fact that you're a sergeant, and I'd get 40 lashes for it, stops me from giving you the beating you deserve," he is alleged to have told his superior. He wouldn't let it lie and returned 15 minutes later with his rifle and shot Jones dead.

SUNDAY 30th MARCH 1958

Bretonside Bus Station came into use. According to the next day's *Western Evening Herald*, Eric Watson, of the Esplanade, was the first person to use the new facility. In fact, he was the only person to board the 5.05am Western National service 88 to Ivybridge on his way to work at Moorhaven Hospital.

FRIDAY 30th MARCH 2001

HMS Cambridge was decommissioned. Cambridge was a Royal Navy shore establishment at Wembury, formerly known as 'HM Gunnery School, Devonport', then 'Cambridge Gunnery School'. It was re-christened after a ship of the same name – an 80-gun third rate ship of the line – that was used to train seamen in gunnery in Plymouth Harbour from 1856. She was replaced by the first rate HMS *Windsor Castle* before the gunnery school was moved on to land at the Plymouth naval barracks in 1907. In 1940, Cambridge Gunnery School, a range for the Army and Navy, was opened at the old Wembury Point Holiday Camp, eventually becoming HMS Cambridge.

FRIDAY 31st MARCH 1995

The Royal Naval Hospital was closed. It had been built during the Seven Years War on a 24-acre site on Stonehouse Creek. It was primarily accessible by water and completed in 1762. Upon closure, the surgeons and nurses were amalgamated with the city's main hospital at Derriford, where they now treat civilians as well as naval and military personnel.

TUESDAY 31st MARCH 2009

Royal Navy bomb disposal experts visited a house in Plymouth to deal with firework-like devices discovered following the arrest of five people who police believed were planning to take part in demonstrations when world leaders arrived for a G20 summit on the financial crisis later in the week. Detectives said a search of one suspect's houses in Plymouth had uncovered several imitation firearms, improvised explosives made of fireworks and material 'relating to political ideology'. "As a precautionary measure, Royal Navy bomb disposal experts will be visiting the premises to ensure the devices are made safe," police said.

APRIL

TUESDAY 1st APRIL 1924

A ceremony to mark the end of five toll-gates on Plymouth's roads saw a phalanx of cars, led by Mayor Solomon Stephens, embark from the Guildhall for a drive which took in each gate: Laira Bridge, the southern and northern gates on the Embankment, Millbridge, and Stonehouse Bridge. The procession halted at each to allow Mayor Stephens to 'declare this road free to the public of Plymouth forever', and lead his newly liberated motorised Plymothians through the gates.

THURSDAY 1st APRIL 1937

The Guinness Clock ticked into action at Drake Circus (as in 'an open circular place where several streets intersect', rather than 'a public entertainment consisting typically of a variety of performances by acrobats, clowns, and trained animals'). The clock, atop the Liverpool Victoria Friendly Society building, had a diameter of 10 feet and was flanked by 'Guinness' on one side and 'Time' on the other, in green. Underneath, was the familiar, but ultimately outlawed, declaration that 'Guinness is good for you', which lit up, one word at a time, in red.

MONDAY 1st APRIL 1974/WEDNESDAY 1st APRIL 1998

When a 1971 Local Government White Paper that proposed abolishing county boroughs was published, Plymouth faced the prospect of being run by a county council 40 miles away in Exeter, a smaller city. Plymouth lobbied – unsuccessfully – for the creation of a Tamarside county comprising Plymouth, Saltash, Torpoint and the surrounding area, before its county borough status was rescinded in 1974 and Devon County Council assumed responsibility for education, social services, highways and libraries. However, Plymouth became a unitary authority in 1998 and all powers returned to the city.

SUNDAY 2nd APRIL 1587

Sir Francis Drake sailed from Plymouth to Cadiz and Corunna where he famously 'singed the King of Spain's beard'. He did not actually go anywhere near the facial hair of Philip II, who, angry at 'El Draque's' piracy against the Spanish in the New World, was planning for an invasion of England. Drake did, though, sail a fleet into two key Spanish ports, occupy the harbours, destroy nearly 40 naval and merchant ships, and thereby delay Philip's Armada for a year.

FRIDAY 3rd APRIL 1896

Pioneer of desert exploration Brigadier Ralph Bagnold was born, in Devonport. Bagnold was the founder and first commander of the British Army's Long Range Desert Group during World War II and penned the influential book *The Physics of Blown Sand and Desert Dune* in 1941, which is still a go-to reference work and was used by NASA in studying sand dunes on Mars. His sister Enid Bagnold wrote the 1935 novel *National Velvet*. Which is probably an easier read.

SATURDAY 4th APRIL 1818

Plymouth-based Parliamentarian Hugh Fortescue was born. The third Earl Fortescue was known as Viscount Ebrington in 1841 when the electorate of Plymouth returned him to the House of Commons. He served as a Whig Lord of the Treasury and Parliamentary Secretary to the Poor Law Board before the same electorate failed to endorse him in 1852. Two years later, he was back in Westminster as the member for Marylebone, a seat he held until 1859, when he was called up to the House of Lords.

THURSDAY 5th APRIL 1621

John Carver died, six months after setting sail from Plymouth to lead the Pilgrims to the New World. The man who chartered the *Mayflower* was a wealthy London merchant who played a crucial part in securing financial support for a colony in America where the Pilgrims could enjoy freedom from religious persecution they experienced in Europe. On arrival in the New World, Carver was elected governor of Plymouth colony and made a treaty of alliance with Chief Massasoit of the Wampanoag tribe. He died soon afterwards, apparently from sunstroke. Nearly 400 years later, Plymouth Argyle employed a coach called John Carver.

MONDAY 6th APRIL 1942

Henry, Duke of Gloucester, made a private Bank Holiday Monday visit to Plymouth. During World War II, the Duke and Duchess of Gloucester worked hard – he usually visited troops, while she toured hospitals – but the purpose of this visit was neither. If it had been to pop down for a loaf of white bread, he would have been unlucky – that item had been available in Plymouth on Easter Sunday for the last time, until after the conflict.

WEDNESDAY 7th APRIL 1784

Naval men Admiral John MacBride and Captain Robert Fanshawe were both elected as Members of Parliament for Plymouth. MacBride saw service during the Seven Years War and the American War of Independence before entering Westminster life. After becoming an MP, he fought in the French Revolutionary Wars and became an Admiral of the Blue shortly before his death in 1800. His name lives on in the Barbican's Admiral MacBride pub, beneath which the original Mayflower Steps are supposedly buried. Fanshawe was a career naval officer and Naval Commissioner of Plymouth from 1797 until his death in 1823. He has several place-names in Alaska named after him. No pub, though.

THURSDAY 8th APRIL 1982

42 Commando left their Bickleigh barracks to sail to the Falklands on board SS *Canberra*. The Royal Marines' part in the conflict later saw them secure Mount Harriet against strong Argentine resistance and continuous artillery bombardment. More than 30 enemy were killed, 300 prisoners taken and 42 Commando suffered two fatalities. For their bravery, the battalion was awarded a Distinguished Service Order, a Military Cross, and four Military Medals. In addition, eight men were mentioned in dispatches.

THURSDAY 9th APRIL 1992

David Jamieson was elected the Labour Member of Parliament for Plymouth Devonport, a seat he retained until standing down in 2005. A teacher, he was senior vice-principal of the John Kitto Community College in Plymouth from 1981 until his election. He was a government whip before becoming Parliamentary Under-Secretary in the Department for Transport in 2001 until his retirement from national politics.

THURSDAY 10th APRIL 2008

Accidents at work cost Plymouth £4.3 million a year, according to figures released on this day. The statistics, released by the Health and Safety Executive, coincided with the launch of a 'Shattered Lives' campaign, created to drive home the importance of safety at work. In the previous 12 months in Plymouth, there had been 272 incidents of trips, slips and falls. Rachel Harris, senior environmental health officer for Plymouth City Council, said some inspections left her shocked and pointed out the highest risk workplaces were in catering, construction and care homes.

MONDAY 11th APRIL 1859

American entrepreneur and entertainer Phineas Taylor Barnum, 'PT' of circus and musical fame, lectured members of the Plymouth Mechanics' Institute on 'The Science of Money Making' at their Princess Square headquarters. Key to his 'science' was the successful selling of what he called 'humbugs' – essentially frauds – such as Joice Heth, claimed to be a 161-year-old slave and nanny to George Washington; the Fejee Mermaid, supposedly a creature with a fish's body and tail, the breasts of an orang-utan, and the head of a baboon; the Wooley Horse, a small maneless horse with woolly hair, described by Barnum as a new species that seemed to be part deer, camel, horse, buffalo, and sheep. The public lapped them up. Barnum also gave talks at St George's Hall, in Stonehouse, and the Devonport Mechanics' Institute, in Duke Street.

MONDAY 11th APRIL 1859

Six years after the laying of the foundation-stone for the Royal Albert Railway Bridge over the River Tamar, the first test train, a South Devon Locomotive, crossed from Plymouth to Saltash.

WEDNESDAY 12th APRIL 1933

The first commercial airline service began from Roborough Airport, with two daily return flights from Plymouth to Cardiff, via Exeter's Haldon Hill aerodrome. The day's first flight, somewhat confusingly operated by Great Western Railway, left Cardiff at 9.15am, called in at Haldon at 10.10am, and arrived at Plymouth at 10.35am. It was turned round in time for an 11.25am return, with an ETA at Cardiff of 12.50pm. The afternoon schedule started at 1.45pm (ETA Plymouth: 3.05pm), with the return leaving Roborough at 3.55pm (ETA Cardiff: 5.20pm). Each three-engined plane held just six passengers and the cost of a Cardiff to Plymouth ticket was £3 10 shillings single, or £6 return.

WEDNESDAY 12th APRIL 1995

The Royal Naval Hospital Unit at Derriford Hospital, otherwise known as 'Stonehouse Ward', was opened by Vice-Chief of the Defence Staff, Air Chief Marshal Sir John Willis KCB CBE RAF. The unit, manned by doctors and nurses from the military services, replaced the Royal Naval Hospital at Stonehouse.

WEDNESDAY 13th APRIL 1768

Lieutenant-General Benjamin Bloomfield, Member of Parliament for Plymouth from 1812-1818, was born. During his time in Westminster, he was made a Privy Councillor and became a Private Secretary to the Sovereign, George IV – having previously been a trusted confidante of the Prince Regent – before falling into disfavour and resigning. He was also a Receiver of the Duchy of Cornwall.

FRIDAY 14th APRIL 1615

The Hospital of the Orphan's Aid was granted a site by Plymouth Corporation in Catherine Street, opposite the west end of St Andrew's Church. William Laurence, a merchant from Vauxhall Street was the hospital's founder, having left £100 in his will to merchants Thomas and Nicholas Sherwill which was put towards almshouses for the poor and educating deprived children and orphans.

TUESDAY 15th APRIL 1975

Plymouth Argyle were promoted to the Second Division when a goal from Paul Mariner in the 50th minute achieved a 1-0 win over Colchester at Home Park. Mariner later left Plymouth to forge an impressive international career with England, playing for Arsenal, Ipswich and Portsmouth, and much later returned to Argyle as the club's head coach.

SUNDAY 16th APRIL 1911

Cold War spy Guy Burgess was born at Albemarle Villas, Devonport. Burgess, along with Donald Maclean, Anthony Blunt and Kim Philby, became a secret supporter of the Communist Party while at Cambridge University and, by 1934, was an agent of the Soviet Union. He maintained this role while working for the BBC, the Press Department of the Foreign Office, as personal assistant to Minister of State for Foreign Affairs Hector McNeil, and at the British embassy in Washington. In 1951, Philby warned Burgess that MI5 was investigating his activities so he and Maclean defected to the USSR, resurfacing in Moscow in 1956. He died from alcohol-related illnesses in 1963, aged 52.

TUESDAY 16th APRIL 1963

Master of the Rolls Lord Denning opened the Law Courts in Armada Way. The County and Crown Court buildings were designed by City Architect Hector Stirling.

MONDAY 17th APRIL 1978

Brittany Ferries' Plymouth-Santander route opened, with *Armorique* making the crossing. The trip from Plymouth reduced the sailing time to 24 hours, which was a much more attractive proposition than the 37-hour journey between Southampton and Spain. In the right conditions, travel time has been trimmed by a further six hours since. In 2008, 169,000 passengers travelled between Plymouth and Santander; the following year, with just one sailing a week, 82,000 passengers made the trip.

FRIDAY 18th APRIL 1589

The English Armada, aka 'the Counter Armada', aka 'the Drake-Norris Expedition', set sail from Plymouth as Queen Elizabeth tried to take advantage of Spain's naval weakness following the earlier failure of the Spanish Armada. The expedition, led by Sir Francis Drake and Sir John Norris (or 'Norreys'), aimed to: raze the Spanish Atlantic fleet, raise a revolt in Lisbon against Philip II, establish a base in the Azores, and seize the Spanish treasure fleet as it returned from America to Cadiz. The fleet was made up of six royal galleons, 60 English armed merchantmen, 60 Dutch flyboats, and 20 pinnaces. On board were 19,000 troops, 4,000 sailors, and 1,500 officers and gentlemen adventurers. The expedition was a naval disaster. There were no takers in Lisbon, the Spanish were ready for a fight, and Drake and Norris lost dozens of ships and thousands of men before limping back to a not terribly chuffed Queen.

SATURDAY 19th APRIL 1913

A small unexploded bomb was discovered by Smeaton's Tower on Plymouth Hoe. It was part of a campaign by suffragettes which also saw devices placed at Prime Minister David Lloyd George's weekend cottage, beside the Coronation Chair in Westminster Abbey, and near the Bank of England. The campaign fizzled out after the beginning of World War I.

THURSDAY 19th APRIL 1962

Plymouth Zoo was opened in Central Park by the Deputy Lord Mayor of Plymouth, William Thompson. Next to Plymouth Argyle's Home Park ground, the zoo contained, amongst other attractions, giraffes, elephants, sea-lions and bears. Such was the interest that the zoo admitted almost 1,000 visitors in its first hour and 13,000 in its first three days, at a cost of one shilling and sixpence for adults and one shilling for children.

SATURDAY 20th APRIL 1957

The *Mayflower II* sailed from Plymouth, England, for Plymouth, Massachusetts, with 31 crew headed by Australian mariner Alan Villiers. The copy-ship was constructed in the Brixham shipyard of Uphams using historically-accurate English oak timber, Stockholm tar, hand-forged nails, linen canvas sails and hemp rope… and a generator, two-way radio and a fridge.

FRIDAY 21st APRIL 1911

John Keily became Roman Catholic Bishop of Plymouth. Irishman Keily was ordained as a priest 34 years before he was elevated to the episcopy, a post he held until his death in 1928. St Boniface's Catholic College in Tavistock Road has a House named after him.

MONDAY 22nd APRIL 1895

Plymouth's first evening newspaper, the *Western Evening Herald*, was launched by the proprietors of the *Western Daily Mercury*. After becoming the *Evening Herald* in 1987, the name was changed to the *Herald* in October 2006 when its print deadline time was moved from around 11am to 1am and it ceased to be an evening paper.

TUESDAY 22nd APRIL 1941

Seventy-six people died in the single most destructive moment of the Second World War in Plymouth when an air-raid complex in Portland Square, a large underground community shelter near Drake's Reservoir, received a direct hit. Sixty years later, the incident was commemorated in the naming of a new building at the University of Plymouth. The overall toll of the Luftwaffe's blitz included: nearly every civic building, two shopping centres, eight cinemas, 26 schools, 41 churches, and 3,754 houses. Another 18,398 dwellings were seriously damaged.

SMEATON'S TOWER ON PLYMOUTH HOE, WHERE AN UNEXPLODED SUFFRAGETTE BOMB WAS ONCE DISCOVERED

WEDNESDAY 23rd APRIL 1941

Millbay Railway Station – the original Plymouth station – was closed after bombs destroyed the nearby goods depot. It was used for passenger trains from 1849 – when it was the only station in the city – until 1941. The South Devon Railway had initially planned to run its broad gauge railway from Exeter to a temporary station at Laira, but had a rethink and extended it to the station between Union Street and Millbay.

SATURDAY 24th APRIL 1591

Sir Francis Drake finished his public work of bringing fresh water into Plymouth from Dartmoor when the watercourse known as 'Plymouth Leat' – sometimes called 'Drake's Leat' – was opened after being blessed by the Rector of Meavy. Legend has it that Drake rode ahead of the cascading water astride a white charger all the way into Plymouth. If indeed he did, he had reason for his triumphalism; the mill into which the leat flowed was leased by Drake, as were all six of the new mills built in the same year, for which he charged £300.

THURSDAY 24th APRIL 1947

Speedway returned to Pennycross Stadium after a decade of inactivity, with the Plymouth Panthers having become the Plymouth Devils in the meantime. Seven years later, the bikes were back in their garages again as the Devils came second best to greyhound and stockcar racing.

SATURDAY 24th APRIL 2004

Goals from Plymothian Michael Evans and Frenchman David Friio saw Plymouth Argyle win the Division Two title at Home Park, where they beat promotion rivals Queens Park Rangers, 2-0. In 2010, after six years in the Championship, under the successive managements of Bobby Williamson, Tony Pulis, Ian Holloway, Paul Sturrock and Paul Mariner, the Pilgrims were relegated back to the third tier of English football. Worse followed when, the following season, Argyle were relegated for the second campaign in succession after entering into a nine-month period of administration which saw them docked ten points by the Football League.

WEDNESDAY 25th APRIL 1821

Career politician and soldier General Henry Lawes Luttrell, Tory Member of Parliament for Plympton Erle between 1790 and 1794, died. Luttrell had already served Bossiney, in Cornwall and Middlesex, as well as sitting in the Irish House of Commons, before he sought the approval of the electorate of Plympton Erle. What would have happened, had he not received it, is debateable. In Middlesex he had been outpolled, by a large margin, by opponent John Wilkes. However, the House of Commons declared that Luttrell 'should have been returned' and seated him. He does not appear to be one of the most popular people all round. Later in his life, when the *Dublin Post* published a retraction for erroneously reporting his death, they headlined it 'Public Disappointment'.

THURSDAY 26th APRIL 1962/FRIDAY 26th APRIL 2002

The Tamar Road Bridge between Plymouth and Saltash was formally opened by the Queen Mother in 1962. After a ceremony involving a fly-past and two naval frigates, Her Majesty cut a tape on the Plymouth side and walked across the bridge to meet the Mayor of Saltash. Between 1998 and 2001, the bridge was strengthened and widened to ensure adequate load-carrying capacity for the future, adding an additional traffic lane and a dedicated pedestrian and cycle lane. Forty years to the day after it was first officially opened, the bridge was officially reopened (although it was never totally closed) by the Queen Mother's granddaughter, the Princess Royal, Princess Anne.

SATURDAY 26th APRIL 2003

Plymouth Albion played their final game at Beacon Park before moving to the Brickfields. A crowd of 2,780 saw them beat Otley 50-13 in National League One before they made way for 95 Wimpey homes. Albion's first home, in the 1870s, had been a pretty primitive Devonport Park, to which players and officials had to carry the goalposts and flags for the game. A lack of facilities meant players had to return home for a bath after the match. Albion then played at Bladderly before, in the 1894 season, moving to Home Park, now the home of Plymouth Argyle, then to Rectory Fields. After World War I, the Navy bought the Rectory for the Devonport Services club and Albion moved to Beacon Park.

THURSDAY 27th APRIL 1944

A plan for Plymouth was published. The City Council had
appointed city planner Sir Patrick Abercrombie and Plymouth
City Engineer and Surveyor James Paton Watson to design a
new Plymouth following the devastation of the city in World
War II. They first had to lobby Parliament to pass a law allowing
them to compulsorily purchase land owned by a wide variety of
disparate owners that had been devastated by the war, and the
resultant slums – and the Town and Country Planning Act was
passed in 1944. The plan divided the suburbs into 'neighbourhood
units', each surrounding a centre containing schools, a church,
a library, a swimming pool, a cinema, a restaurant, a laundry,
and a community building, gathered together in a precinct. The
city centre was divided into several precincts, each with its own
function; shopping, civic centre, offices, theatres, recreation and
culture, with the Barbican labelled 'historic Plymouth'. The old
streets were replaced with wide, modern boulevards aligned east
to west, linked by a north-south avenue connecting the railway
station at North Hill and Plymouth Hoe. Armada Way and
Royal Parade were also conceived. The original plan had been
for Royal Parade to line up with Union Street, but that never
happened.

SUNDAY 28th APRIL 1912

Survivors of the *Titanic* shipwreck landed at Millbay Docks in
secrecy. Early in the day, the SS *Lapland* moored at Cawsand Bay
with the 167 *Titanic* passengers who had not been detained in New
York for an inquiry. A tender, the *Sir Richard Grenville*, delayed
coming alongside at West Hoe while dock labourers and porters
were paid off and escorted out. The survivors were then allowed to
disembark before being put on a train to Southampton.

WEDNESDAY 29th APRIL 1959

Plymouth Argyle won promotion to the Second Division of the
Football League after a 1-1 draw against Bradford City at Home
Park. Wilf Carter scored the goal that gave the Pilgrims the Third
Division championship in the first season after the amalgamation
of the north and south sections of the division.

SATURDAY 29th APRIL 1961

Westward Television started broadcasting from a transmitter near Honiton. There was no opening ceremony, just networked programmes until 11pm, when *Hello from Westward* was shown, followed by a local *Epilogue* from the Bishop of Exeter. The chairman of the company was Peter Cadbury, who named the company after a golf course in Westward Ho! where he played. Westward were based at Derry's Cross, where they had three studios built at a cost of more than £500,000.

TUESDAY 29th APRIL 1986

Home Park witnessed another Plymouth Argyle promotion to the Second Division with a 4-0 victory over Bristol City. Tommy Tynan scored twice, and Garry Nelson and Russell Coughlin – direct from a corner-kick – netted one apiece to start the celebrations.

THURSDAY 30th APRIL 1981

Actress Emma Pierson was born in Plymouth. Best known for her role as Anna Thornton-Wilton in the British television drama *Hotel Babylon*, she is the daughter of a nurse and a Royal Navy submariner.

SUNDAY 30th APRIL 1944

Luftwaffe bombers paid a final World War II visit to Plymouth and left their mark on the city's waterfront, with 18 people killed in the Oreston area as a public shelter took a direct hit. The city had not suffered an air-raid since the end of the previous year. As well as the waterfront carnage, the Western National Omnibus Company took a strike, with three firewatchers killed and buses destroyed by fire, and the Rising Sun pub at Crabtree was badly damaged.

MAY

FRIDAY 1st MAY 1818

The foundation-stone of the original Athenaeum, home to the Plymouth Institution for the promotion of Science, Literature and the Liberal Arts, was laid in Derry's Cross. The stone was laid by the Institution's founder, and former Mayor of Plymouth, Henry Woollcombe and the Athenaeum was the last of its several homes, which included; a room in Woolster Street, a committee room of the Public Library, and a room at the Fine Art Gallery in Frankfort Street.

SATURDAY 1st MAY 1830

The Royal Union Baths were opened situated off Union Road – later Union Street – having been granted a Royal Charter to allow the erection of 'commodious baths for the accommodation, comfort and convenience of the inhabitants and visitors of Plymouth'. Two large swimming baths, one for men and one for women, were housed, each with 12 dressing-rooms. There were also separate baths for children and those with skin diseases. The Baths were demolished 18 years later in favour of the new South Devon Railway terminus at Millbay.

MONDAY 2nd MAY 1859

The Royal Albert Bridge was opened by Prince Albert, who had agreed to it being named after him as early as 1853. He was also invited to perform the opening ceremony and did so after travelling from Windsor on a special train. Several thousand spectators also turned out, but guests from Cornwall were late for the ceremony because their train broke down, and illness prevented designer Isambard Kingdom Brunel's attendance. Brunel died later in the year and his name was placed above the portals at either end of the bridge as a memorial.

SATURDAY 2nd MAY 1964

Nancy Astor, the first woman to sit in the House of Commons, representing Plymouth Sutton, died, aged 84, leaving behind her a string of quotable quotes, such as: "I married beneath me – all women do"; "One reason why I don't drink is because I wish to know when I am having a good time"; "The only thing I like about rich people is their money"; or even "We women talk too much, but even then we don't tell half what we know."

FRIDAY 2nd MAY 1947

Parts of Bickleigh and Tamerton Foliot were officially absorbed into Plymouth as the city expanded after World War II. Confusingly, they remain under the jurisdiction of South Hams District Council.

THURSDAY 3rd MAY 1855

The *John*, a 468-ton sailing ship, left Plymouth bound for Quebec, carrying 268 passengers looking to start a new life in North America. She made it as far as the Manacle Rocks, St Keverne, Cornwall, before sinking with the loss of 194 lives, although captain Edward Rawle and his 19 crew all survived. In 1848, 89 ships left Plymouth with 8,505 emigrants aboard; by 1849, it had risen to 130 ships carrying 15,895 people, of which 109 ships (14,118 people) went to Australia, and 10 ships (1,171 emigrants) headed for Canada.

SATURDAY 3rd MAY 1941

Following the latest Luftwaffe blitz on the city, around 650 schoolchildren were evacuated to north Cornwall on board a special train from Plymouth's Friary Station.

WEDNESDAY 4th MAY 1859

An Act of Parliament authorised the South Devon Railway to build a branch from Millbay to Devonport which would have been very convenient for the dockyards. However, the powers were subsequently transferred to the Cornwall Railway, who came up with plans for a broad-gauge line that would cross the River Tamar on the Torpoint Ferry. The ambitious designs were thrown out by Parliament, so Isambard Kingdom Brunel designed the Royal Albert Bridge to carry the line instead.

WEDNESDAY 5th MAY 1982

The current Theatre Royal, on Royal Parade, was officially opened by Princess Margaret. Designed by the Peter Moro Partnership, it is the third incarnation of the theatre which was originally at the top of George Street and known as the 'Theatre, Frankfort-Gate', before it adopted the name 'Theatre Royal' after King George III and his family visited it in 1789. The second Theatre Royal was at the other end of George Street and existed between 1813 and 1937, when it became a victim of the popularity of cinema and was demolished.

WEDNESDAY 6th MAY 1885

Lawyer Roundell Palmer, twice Lord Chancellor of Great Britain, died. Selborne entered Parliament as a Peelite Conservative Member of Parliament for Plymouth in 1847 and represented the constituency for ten of the next 11 years. He served as Solicitor General between 1861 and 1863 and as Attorney General between 1863 and 1866. Under William Gladstone, he became Lord Chancellor in 1872, seeing through the 1873 Judicature Act which completely reorganised the judiciary. He served in the same office in Gladstone's second Cabinet from 1880.

WEDNESDAY 6th MAY 1998

The National Marine Aquarium was opened in Rope Walk, Coxside. Extended in 2002, it boasts 50 live exhibits, including three massive tanks, the largest of which – Britain's deepest – holds 2.5m litres of water. More than 4,000 animals from 400 species are displayed in realistic habitats, from local shorelines to coral reefs.

MONDAY 6th MAY 1935

"The King, on the recommendation of the Home Secretary, has been graciously pleased to command that in commemoration of His Majesty's Silver Jubilee, the Chief Magistrate, now and for the time being, of the City of Plymouth, shall bear the style and title Lord Mayor." – King George V, in commemoration of his Silver Jubilee, granted the dignity of Lord Mayor to the city of Plymouth; James Elliott Pillar became the first person to hold the office; and the city has had a Lord Mayor ever since.

FRIDAY 7th MAY 1948

The last German prisoners of war, who had been kept in Second World War POW camps in and around Plymouth, were sent off to Suffolk to be repatriated. The Chaddlewood House camp, in Plympton, from which they were escorted, was the South Devon headquarters for all POW camps.

TUESDAY 7th MAY 1895

English architect of the Victorian era James Piers St Aubyn, died. J P specialised in church architecture and was responsible for the design of five in Devonport; St Paul's (1851); St James the Less (1851); St Mary's (1852) and St Stephen's (1852); and St Barnabas (unknown).

TUESDAY 8th MAY 1990

A dredger working near the Torpoint Ferry brought up an unexploded 500lb wartime bomb. The bomb was taken a mile south of the Breakwater before being blown up by the Royal Navy Bomb Disposal team.

WEDNESDAY 9th MAY 1906

The Co-op Bakery at Beacon Park was opened in some style – more than 160 decorated Co-op vans, trolleys and floats processed through the Three Towns before reaching the new premises. After the doors were opened with a ceremonial golden key, more than 10,000 locals were given a guided tour of the impressive new facility.

THURSDAY 10th MAY 1956

The new premises of Spooner & Company Ltd in Royal Parade were officially opened by Lady Astor. It was 112 years earlier that Joseph Spooner had come to Plymouth and set up a linen and woollen drapery business in Whimple Street. In 1971, Spooner & Company Ltd merged with John Yeo & Company Ltd, whose parent company's name was given to the store – Debenham's.

FRIDAY 11th MAY 1945

Plymouth's street lights were switched back on for the first time since the beginning of World War II.

MONDAY 11th MAY 2009

The largest oyster recorded in British waters was dredged up off Plymouth. 'Shelly'(!) was discovered at the bottom of a box of mixed fish bought by a Cornish fishmonger Peter Randall at the city's fish-market. Peter donated the 3lb monster – getting on for twice the size of Britain's previous biggest oyster – to Mevagissey Sealife Aquarium in south Cornwall. "It's just huge," he said. "I thought it would be a shame to kill it. You certainly couldn't eat it all in one go, anyway."

TUESDAY 11th MAY 1971

Prog rock outfit King Crimson recorded a live album at the Guildhall. Titled *Live at Plymouth Guildhall* (no, really), the two-CD set was released through the King Crimson Collectors' Club in January 2001 after being adapted from the original soundboard tape and an audience bootleg.

THURSDAY 12th MAY 1988

Canadian sculptor and artist Rick Gibson was arrested in Plymouth after pushing a pram around the city centre containing live slugs, snails, worms, beetles and other bugs. He then invited Plymothians to select one... and kill it with insecticide. Gibson called it; "A little performance piece that explored people's desire to kill living things." Other performance art by the nutty North American included standing in front of the Director of Public Prosecutions office in London with a live rat in front of his face. Better than a dead one, I guess.

FRIDAY 13th MAY 2005

Anti-nuclear weapons protestors occupied Drake's Island in Plymouth Sound and declared it a nuclear-free state. The protest – against the refit of the UK's nuclear armed and nuclear powered Trident submarines in Devonport Dockyard – coincided with an important nuclear disarmament conference at the United Nations in New York.

MONDAY 14th MAY 1973

Rugby union international Julian White was born in Plymouth. Tight-head prop White followed in his father's studmarks by playing for Plymouth Albion, as well as Salcombe and Kingsbridge, before making his name with Leicester Tigers. One of the most powerful forwards in the game in his time, and a feared scrummager, he won 46 England caps and represented the British Lions on their tour to New Zealand in 2005.

SUNDAY 15th MAY 1977

Punk came to Plymouth's Fiesta Suite in Mayflower Street in the shape of The Buzzcocks, Slits, Subway Sect and 'White Riot Tour' headliners The Clash, who played a 16-song set or, more accurately, a 15-song set in which '1977' was played twice, the second time as a 75-second encore. The Clash were making a quick return to the city having supported the Sex Pistols, on their notorious 'Anarchy in the UK' tour at Woods Club the previous December. Highlight of the gig, of which a bootleg recording still exists, is their version of Junior Murvin and Lee 'Scratch' Perry's *Police and Thieves* which includes some improvised lyrics from vocalist Joe Strummer towards the end of the song: "Walking down Plymouth High Street... maybe in the Navy... Vietnam... nothing going on in Plymouth."

FRIDAY 16th MAY 1828

General Sir William Congreve, Member of Parliament for Plymouth between 1818 and 1828, died in office, aged 55. Congreve was better known as an inventor, specifically for the development and deployment of pioneering Congreve rockets, weapons which paved the way for future military developments that made a tremendous impact on modern warfare. His rockets were essentially incendiaries made up of layers of sheet iron. A hollow iron head was developed which could be loaded with shell or rounds; the larger types could house musket balls with a charge behind them. In 1811, Sir William was elected Fellow of the Royal Society, following which he invented a hydro-pneumatic lock that has been used on canals since, and patented improvements to the manufacture of bank-note paper to prevent forgery. His name lives on in Congreve Gardens, Manadon.

MONDAY 17th MAY 1954

Laurel & Hardy appeared on stage in Plymouth just once. In fact, they appeared for just one night of their scheduled week. Stan and Ollie were booked to play the last shows of their 'Birds of a Feather' British tour on the same Palace Theatre bill as, among others, Harry Worth and 'Wonder Horse Tony'. Unfortunately, Ollie was in a fine mess with severe flu, which may have contributed to his mild heart attack that saw the show cancelled.

THURSDAY 18th MAY 1876

Devonport Railway Station received its first passengers when London and South Western Railway trains arrived on time. The station – then called 'Devonport and Stonehouse' – was a large building facing Paradise Road near the junction with Kings Road. The 'and Stonehouse' was dropped from the name quite early on, and, from 26th September 1949, the station was known as 'Devonport Kings Road' in order to distinguish it from the Western Region station at Devonport Albert Road. The station closed on September 7th 1964 when the remaining trains were diverted over the Western Region route to St Budeaux, but goods traffic continued until March 7th 1971. The station was demolished and the City College Plymouth has been built on the site although it lives on in the shape of the Paradise Road wall, which is topped by the London and South Western Railway's decorative railings.

SATURDAY 19th MAY 1923

The Plymouth War Memorial was unveiled by the Secretary of State for War, the Right Honourable Earl of Derby, to remember those who had died in what was then known as the Great War – World War I. The memorial, at the junction of Lockyer Street and Citadel Road, now also serves as a commemoration to the dead of World War II.

MONDAY 19th MAY 1975

The golden age of Plymouth commercial radio began when Plymouth Sound 261 was launched with Cat Stevens' *Morning Has Broken*, the first record played on the breakfast show, 'Sunrise Sound', presented by Colin Bower. David Bassett and Louise Churchill were also on air on day one of the new station, which also hosted the likes of Mike Allen, Ian Calvert, Peter Greig, Brian Measures and Gordon Sparks. The golden age had long since passed when Plymouth Sound became part of Heart FM in March 2009.

SATURDAY 20th MAY 1848

The following appeared on the front pages of the *Plymouth Times* and the *Plymouth, Devonport & Stonehouse Herald*: "ALTERATION OF TIME: BOROUGH OF PLYMOUTH: THE COUNCIL of the BOROUGH of PLYMOUTH, considering the Advantage of a Uniform Computation of Time, and following the example of other large Towns possessing communication by Railway, have resolved to adopt LONDON TIME as kept by all Railway Stations in regulating the arrival and departure of Trains. Notice is therefore hereby given that from and after Twelve o'clock at Noon, on MONDAY, the twenty-second day of May instant, London Time, being 16 minutes earlier than Plymouth Time, is appointed to be kept for all purposes within the Borough of Plymouth. JAMES MOORE, Mayor. Guildhall, Plymouth." All aboard!

SATURDAY 21st MAY 1994

World Champion diver Tom Daley was born. Daley started diving with Plymouth Diving Club as a seven-year-old and, seven years later, represented Great Britain at the 2008 Olympics in Beijing, where, aged 14 years and 81 days, he was Britain's youngest competitor and the youngest of any nationality to reach a final. He finished seventh in the individual ten-metre platform dive and eighth in the synchronised event, with Blake Aldridge. Four years later, he won bronze in the ten-metre platform at the London 2012 Olympics.

THURSDAY 21st MAY 2009

Hilary Lister left Plymouth on her way to becoming the first disabled woman to sail solo around Britain. Hilary, who suffers from the progressive condition reflex sympathetic dystrophy and controls her craft by sucking and blowing tubes for steering and sails, had originally embarked on her quest from Dover the previous June. Bad weather and technical problems saw the attempt suspended after two months but she later restarted from Plymouth. She completed her circumnavigation.

FRIDAY 22nd MAY 2009

The second annual Plymouth Volksfest began at Newnham Park. The three-day Volksfest was conceived as an alternative to the Run To The Sun festival held in Newquay, Cornwall, and is essentially a music festival for Volkswagen enthusiasts comprising live bands, DJ sets, and children's entertainment, alongside the usual Show 'n' Shine car displays and car-related activities. Live acts included headliners Stereo MCs, Dreadzone, and Hazel O'Connor.

SUNDAY 23rd MAY 1943

St Andrew's, the mother church of Plymouth, held its first service since it was destroyed by the Luftwaffe raids of March 1941. Only the walls and tower remained after the Nazi battering. Actually, that is not quite true – the walls, the tower and the indomitable spirit of Plymothians remained, as was evidenced by a wooden sign fixed over the north porch door. It contained one word, Resurgam (Latin: I shall rise again), which encapsulated the wartime spirit in the city. It was a motto, not just for St Andrew's, but for the people of Plymouth. Just over two years later, police were obliged to control the crowds as hundreds of people turned out for the service in the risen-again church. The entrance to St Andrew's is still referred to as the 'Resurgam' door and a carved granite plaque is now permanently fixed there.

THURSDAY 23rd MAY 1957

John Betjeman and Al Rowse were among 500 people who attended a meeting at Abbey Hall – the city's second oldest surviving building – to discuss plans for the renovation of the Barbican. Simply, the council wanted "the hovels to come down", while Betjeman, Rowse and their fellow members of the Old Plymouth Society wanted a measure of preservation. Compromise was eventually reached.

SATURDAY 24th MAY 1572

Sir Francis Drake set sail from Plymouth with a crew of 73 men in two small vessels, the *Pascha* and the *Swan*, for Panama – the Spanish Main – where Peruvian treasure was landed before being taken overland to the town of Nombre de Dios and waiting Spanish galleons. It was the first time Drake had taken charge of an expedition and it nearly went horribly wrong. He captured Nombre de Dios but had to leave the treasure behind when he was wounded in battle and his crew insisted on withdrawing to save his life.

SUNDAY 25th MAY 1919

Plymouth staged its first Remembrance Sunday on the Hoe, which consisted of a day-long laying of flowers on the National Armada Memorial. The first of more than 2,000 tributes was placed at 5am by Doctor William Waterfield, whose idea the day had been. "These floral tributes are sacred to the memory of those who laid down their lives to save the Empire," read a notice. "They will remain until faded. Please respect this spot."

WEDNESDAY 25th MAY 1892

Beaumont Park, Plymouth's first public park, was officially opened to Plymothians, who had the vision of the Reverend Thomas Bewes to thank for it. Thomas had inherited Beaumont House and extended its gardens throughout his residence. When, in 1882, he bought a strip of land from fellow priest Sir Michael Culme-Seymour, he stipulated in the deeds that it was to be held until taken over by the Borough of Plymouth with the rest of the park. He was aware that new laws concerned with the health of towns made it possible for local authorities to create recreation areas for citizens who lived in overcrowded accommodation. Following Thomas's death in 1890, his trustees sold the house and park to Plymouth Corporation for £26,000.

SATURDAY 26th MAY 2007

Sir Elton John headlined a sell-out concert at Home Park as 22,000 people enjoyed a two-and-a-half-hour set of 24 songs including 'Rocket Man' and 'Crocodile Rock'. Other acts to have rocked Plymouth Argyle's home since have included George Michael, Meat Loaf, Westlife and Rod Stewart.

THURSDAY 26th MAY 1955

Joan Vickers, later Baroness Vickers of Devonport in the county of Devon, was elected Member of Parliament for Devonport, a seat she held for nearly two decades. Representing the National Liberal Party, she surprisingly won the seat from Michael Foot, but she was a Conservative by the time she lost it in 1974 to another Labour Party heavyweight, Dr David Owen, by just 437 votes. She was created a life peer the following year.

MONDAY 27th MAY 1901

A Whit Monday athletics meeting was the first event staged at Home Park by the Argyle Athletic Club. Home Park was then an oval-shaped bowl and cinder track in the middle of allotments and farmland, but, within two years, it was hosting Plymouth Argyle's first competitive match.

THURSDAY 27th MAY 1999

The Barbican Leisure Park was opened by TV and radio presenter Jonathan Ross and Wonderbra model Caprice. The £40m development on a former Coxside gas works boasted ten-pin bowling, restaurants, bars, nightclubs, a health and fitness suite, and a £15m, 15-screen multiplex cinema, which, on opening night, showed the Hugh Grant film *Notting Hill*.

SUNDAY 28th MAY 1967

At exactly 8.56pm, Francis Chichester sailed his battered ketch *Gipsy Moth IV* past the lighthouse at the western end of Plymouth Breakwater, 274 days after having departed from the city aboard the same craft. He had spent 226 of those days on his own at sea as he became the first person to achieve a true circumnavigation of the world – solo – from west to east via the Great Capes. He covered around 24,000 miles and made only one landing, at Sydney, for repairs. He was accompanied on the last part of his journey by a flotilla of small boats, and a crowd of around 200,000 people packed on to the Hoe and foreshore to honour his return. After a short speech, he attended a formal reception in Plymouth Guildhall. Nine years earlier, Chichester had been diagnosed with terminal lung cancer which had gone into remission after wife-to-be Sheila put him on a strict vegetarian diet.

MONDAY 28th MAY 2007

Gipsy Moth IV completed its second global circumnavigation, 40 years to the day after the first, this time with a crew of three. They were the last of 90 youngsters who crewed for experienced skippers as Sir Francis Chichester's famous boat once more traversed the globe before being welcomed back to Plymouth after a near two-year voyage. They were received by Giles Chichester, son of Sir Francis, at West Hoe Pier, where his father had come ashore in 1967. Among the final crew was 16-year-old Plymothian Grant McCade.

MONDAY 28th MAY 1928

The Greyhound Racing Association (Plymouth) Ltd held its inaugural meeting at Pennycross Stadium with a card comprising four flat and three hurdle races on a track that cost £30,000 and took six months to build. Within a year, Pennycross was staging greyhound meetings every Monday, Wednesday and Saturday.

THURSDAY 29th MAY 1884

Plymouth Promenade Pier was first opened to the public, having cost £45,000. The pier was the idea of tailor Edward Lancaster, who built an edifice that initially included shops, a clock tower and a landing stage. Within ten years, a 2,000-seat pavilion was added for concert parties, roller-skating, band concerts, dancing, boxing and wrestling. Following these halcyon days, the pier, which was one of the first public places in Plymouth to be lit by electricity, struggled financially, and, in 1938, receivers were called in. No buyer had been found before the pier was bombed beyond use during World War II. The War Damage Commission bought out debenture holders and agreed to pay the £4,754 demolition costs.

THURSDAY 30th MAY 1895

St Andrew's Cross was dedicated, having been erected as a memorial to the graveyard next to St Andrew's Church which had been levelled. The 70ft edifice was designed by James Hine of Hine and Odgers, Lockyer Street, and erected by John Finch, of York Road. After being badly damaged during the Plymouth blitz of 1941, it was broken up; two statues – *Lady with Child* and *Peace with Dove'* – were transferred to the Guildhall, while the bronze cross that topped the original found a home on St Andrew's Church altar.

MONDAY 30th MAY 1825

The Plymouth Mechanics' Institute was formed: "For the voluntary association of mechanics and others, and the payment of a small weekly sum; donations of money, books, specimens, implements, models, and apparatus; a library of reference, a circulating library, and a reading room; a museum of machines, models, minerals, and natural history; lectures on natural and experimental philosophy, practical mechanics, astronomy, chemistry, literature, and the arts; an experimental workshop and laboratory originating with the members." If you had not worked it out, Mechanics' Institutes were educational establishments formed to provide adult education, particularly in technical subjects, to working men. Plymouth's working men wound up their Mechanics' Institute in 1898.

SATURDAY 31st MAY 1919

RAF Cattewater (HQ: Mount Wise Barracks) briefly became the epicentre of the aviation world when a Curtiss NC flying-boat, imaginatively named the NC-4, landed there. The American plane had, four days earlier, become the first craft to fly across the Atlantic when it landed at Lisbon, Portugal. The crossing from Naval Air Station Rockaway, New York, had taken 19 days, as they put down at Chatham Naval Air Station, Nova Scotia, Newfoundland, and the Azores, before making Lisbon. It then flew on to England, arriving at RAF Mount Batten to great fanfare. The NC4 had originally been accompanied by the NC-1 and the NC-3 (but not the NC-2, which had been cannibalised for spares) but both of these were forced to land at sea by foul weather. More than 50 US Navy warships 'strung out like a string of pearls' at 50-mile intervals along the route had helped navigation. After arriving in Plymouth, the crew travelled to London by train and received a tumultuous welcome. While they visited Paris, the NC-4 was dismantled in Plymouth and loaded on the USS *Aroostook* for the return journey to the United States. The reason why we do not, today, hear more about the crew of Albert Read, Walter Hinton, Elmer Stone, James Breese, Eugene Rhoads, and Herbert Rodd is that, less than a month later, Alcock and Brown completed the first non-stop transatlantic flight from Newfoundland to Ireland.

JUNE

SUNDAY 1st JUNE 1924

Queen Marie of Rumania was welcomed to Plymouth by Mayor Solomon Stephens, with whom she reminisced about the city. The Queen was the eldest daughter of Prince Alfred, previously the Royal Navy's Commander-in-Chief. "I have returned... with the simple purpose of visiting again the places where so many happy days of my childhood were spent," she said.

THURSDAY 1st JUNE 1967

The City of Plymouth police were amalgamated with Devon and Exeter Police and Cornwall County Constabulary to form the Devon & Cornwall Constabulary, the largest police force, by area covered, in England.

MONDAY 1st JUNE 1903

Percy Whitlock, composer of the 'Plymouth Suite', was born. Whitlock was an English organist and composer who had been a student of Vaughan Williams at London's Royal College of Music. He wrote the 'Plymouth Suite' after he and his wife Edna had gone on a trip to the city from their home in Kent to attend a conference of the Incorporated Association of Organists. There are five movements, each of which is dedicated to an organist who had attended the conference.

FRIDAY 2nd JUNE 1609

The *Sea Venture*, the new flagship of the Virginia Company, established by James I with the purpose of establishing settlements on the coast of North America, set sail from Plymouth on the so-called 'Third Supply Mission' to Jamestown. The *Sea Venture* led a fleet of eight ships containing 500-600 people, including Admiral Sir George Somers. Two months into the voyage, the fleet ran into a strong storm which split the party. The *Sea Venture* fought for three days before she started to leak badly, largely as a result of her new timbers not having set. With his crew on the point of collapse and the *Sea Venture* about to sink, Sir George spied land and deliberately drove the ship on to the reefs, allowing all 150 people aboard – and one dog – to be landed safely ashore on what turned out to be Bermuda... which he then claimed for the crown. The wrecking of the *Sea Venture* is widely thought to have been the inspiration for Shakespeare's *The Tempest*.

FRIDAY 3rd JUNE 1904

'Buffalo Bill', or to give him his full name, Colonel William Cody, visited Plymouth as part of his 'Wild West Show and Congress of Rough Riders of the World Absolutely Final Tour of Britain'. Bill moseyed into town from Bodmin on one of three special trains which also contained 1,300 men and women, 800 show horses, and their associated paraphernalia. The American showman gave the Westcountry his unique take on the Wild West in two shows at the Exhibition Fields, Pennycomequick. They featured performers from South America, the Middle East and Japan, but basically it was a huge game of cowboys and what are now known, rightly, as native Americans. It was popular, though. As the *Evening Herald* reported; "For the benefit of the country visitors, the Great Western Railway will run a late special train, which will leave Millbay at 10.55 pm calling at North-Road and Mutley for Plymstock, Billacombe, Elburton Cross, Brixton Road, Steer Point and Yealmpton."

THURSDAY 3rd JUNE 1824

George IV gave his royal assent to the Act of Parliament which authorised the purchase of 16 acres of land at 'Cremill Point' for the building of a victualling, or supply, depot for the Royal Navy. It was the making of East Stonehouse as workers at the depot – from shipwrights to grocers – settled in the area near their work.

FRIDAY 3rd JUNE 1960

The foundation-stone of the Plymstock Shopping Centre was laid by Sir George Hater-Hames, the chairman of Devon County Council, who said that the scheme would make Plymstock "an individual place that would not be absorbed by that place across the river". On 1st April 1967, Plymstock, along with Plympton, was absorbed into the city of Plymouth.

SUNDAY 4th JUNE 2000

Solo long-distance yachtswoman Ellen MacArthur left Plymouth in her monohull *Kingfisher*: 14 days, 23 hours, 11 minutes later, she arrived in Newport, Rhode Island, on the other side of the Atlantic. At the time of writing, it is the record for a single-handed monohull east-to-west passage, and the record for a single-handed woman in any vessel.

SATURDAY 4th JUNE 1881

The Devonport Mechanics' Institute shut down after 56 years. Its Duke Street premises and collection of some 11,000 books were bought by Devonport Corporation for £2,500. It did not take the greatest leap of the imagination to utilise the contents and building by re-opening it as the Devonport Library the following year.

MONDAY 5th JUNE 1944

Thousands of American troops – the majority the US 29th Armoured Division – boarded landing craft from the slipways of the Torpoint Ferry, and at Jupiter Point, Cremyll, Turnchapel, Saltash Passage and Barn Pool, in Mount Edgcumbe, to be taken to ships bound for Normandy's beaches. It proved to be a false start as the hundreds of vessels of various shapes and sizes were beaten back by bad weather and had to return to Plymouth. They went again the following day and eventually landed at the beaches codenamed 'Utah' and 'Omaha'.

SATURDAY 6th JUNE 1868

Explorer Sir Robert Falcon Scott was born at 'Outlands', a small country estate near Stoke Damerel, a distant descendant of Sir Walter Scott. Young 'Con', as he was known to his nearest and dearest, was born into a large family – he had two older sisters, Ettie and Rose, a younger brother, Archie, and a younger sister, Katherine – and was seen as a daydreamer who was queasy at the sight of blood – not exactly credentials for a Royal Navy officer and pioneer. The Scotts had to leave Outlands when the money raised by Scott's father John from the sale of a small brewery in Hoegate Street ran out, but Scott retained a strong association with Plymouth, not least of all through the Navy. Like most of Plymouth, Outlands was bombed to pieces during World War II, following which St Bartholomew's Church was built on the site and, in 1959, consecrated by Bishop of Exeter Dr Robert Mortimer. In the church hall, next to the church, is a large piece of a birch tree on which Scott had carved his name. The celebrated act of vandalism is in a glass case containing the caption: "The name on the bark of this piece of birch was cut by Captain Robert Falcon Scott, RN, at his home, Outlands, Plymouth."

THE BELVEDERE ON PLYMOUTH HOE, WHICH WAS BUILT ON THE FORMER BULL RING

FRIDAY 6th JUNE 1958

The Drake Cinema, just off Derry's Cross roundabout, was opened by Lord Mayor George Wingett, who then settled down with his popcorn and orange squash to watch a Movietone News film *Plymouth Story* and the charity premier of *South Pacific*. It later became the Drake Odeon and boasted an imposing model of the *Golden Hind* over its entrance. It closed on 31st October 1999, when a screening of *Big Daddy* was watched by nine people – a far cry from the 1,600 full-houses of its early days.

WEDNESDAY 7th JUNE 1882

The last political meeting to be held in the Bull Ring on the Hoe took place, as, not long afterwards, a bye-law was passed prohibiting all public meetings on the Hoe except with the permission of the Town Council. The Bull Ring was supplanted in 1890 by the Belvedere but, in the 17th century, all bulls were required to be tethered and baited by bulldogs before being sold to ensure the meat was tender. Butchers would be fined if they failed to bait the bulls.

MONDAY 8th JUNE 1724

John Smeaton, whose name is destined to be part of Plymouth's history because of his tower on the Hoe, was born. A Yorkshire-born civil engineer, Smeaton designed the third Eddystone Lighthouse, having pioneered the use of 'hydraulic lime', a form of mortar which sets under water, and developed a technique involving dovetailed blocks of granite in the building of the lighthouse. He was good, too. His lighthouse lasted for around 120 years at sea before erosion set in to the rocks below it and it was dismantled and partially rebuilt on the Hoe.

FRIDAY 9th JUNE 1893

The Plymouth Corporation Act authorised the construction of Burrator Reservoir. It followed a report from Plymouth's water engineer Edward Sandeman that recommended turning Burrator Gorge into a storage reservoir with a pipeline from there taking water into the town. The reservoir was officially opened a little over five years later by the mayor, John Bond. The cost was £178,000, with another £126,000 being spent on two dams, at Burrator and Sheepstor.

TUESDAY 9th JUNE 1981

Derriford Hospital was officially opened, having cost £22m to build. The initial intake of patients came from Devonport Hospital and they were later joined by others from Greenbank and Freedom Fields hospitals. The first male and female patients – Shirley Jenkins and Fred Hobbs – were presented with bouquets of flowers by staff. Although not fully completed when it opened, there was huge interest in the new building: in the fortnight leading up to the opening, more than 10,000 people were shown around on conducted tours to see the wards, theatres, chapel and kitchens.

SUNDAY 10th JUNE 1860

Plymouth-born soldier and explorer Edmund Lockyer died in Woolloomooloo, Australia. The son of a sailmaker, Lockyer reached the rank of major in the 57th Regiment and, in April 1825, was posted to Sydney, capital of the British Colony of New South Wales for, initially, an exploratory mission. In late 1826, however, with the British government fearful the French were looking to establish a colony on the Australian west coast, Lockyer was asked to lead an expedition to claim Western Australia for Britain. He sailed on the brig *Amity*, arriving at King George Sound on 25th December, with 20 troops and 23 convicts, to begin the first European settlement in Western Australia. The following year, he sold his commission and settled in the colony. He became superintendent of police at Parramatta, then sergeant-at-arms to the Legislative Council in the Parliament of New South Wales; and, in 1856, usher of the black rod.

TUESDAY 11th JUNE 1583

Sir Humphrey Gilbert, 'the father of British Colonisation', set sail from Plymouth Sound for Newfoundland, which he claimed for Queen Elizabeth I two months later, the first English property in North America. An English nobleman, army officer, Member of Parliament for Plymouth and explorer, Gilbert is said to have believed that America was the lost continent of Atlantis. Within weeks of arriving, though, his fleet departed without having tried to form a settlement because of a lack of supplies. Sir Humphrey – a half-brother of Sir Walter Raleigh – went on to explore the area around Nova Scotia before setting out on the return trip, but died when his frigate, the *Squirrel*, sank near the Azores.

WEDNESDAY 12th JUNE 1616

Virginia Indian chief's daughter Pocahontas arrived in Plymouth, en route to London and on the arm of her husband John Rolfe, a colonist. Having assisted settlers at Jamestown, she had embraced Christianity and was baptised 'Rebecca'. After Rolfe and Pocahontas boarded a ship to return to Virginia, Pocahontas became gravely ill. She was taken ashore and died. It is unknown what caused her death, but theories range from smallpox, pneumonia, or tuberculosis, to her having been poisoned.

WEDNESDAY 12th JUNE 1935

Multi Oscar-winning American film producer Walt Disney cruised into Plymouth aboard the French liner *Normandie*, which was making its first voyage from New York to the city, in a record time for the crossing of four days, 11 hours, and 42 minutes. Walt and his wife Lillian then took the boat train to Paddington, where they were mobbed by a crowd so enthusiastic that children had to be rescued from the crush. Sounds to me like the security arrangements were a bit Mickey Mouse.

SATURDAY 13th JUNE 1931

The first speedway meeting in Plymouth was held at the Pennycross Stadium track as around 6,000 people watched Plymouth Tigers beat Exeter 32-21. The Tigers entered the National League between 1932 and 1934 and Pennycross hosted some of the best riders in the world, like Vic Huxley, Frank Arthur, Jack Palmer and Bluey Wilkinson, but crowds had dwindled so much by 1937 that racing ceased until after World War II. Pennycross Stadium was demolished in 1972.

MONDAY 14th JUNE 1875

Politician Freddie Guest, Member of Parliament for Plymouth Drake between 1931 and 1937, was born. Guest was a first cousin of Winston Churchill, who he followed from the Conservative Party to the Liberals and into the House of Commons as MP for East Dorset. He took a break from politics to serve in World War I, winning the Distinguished Service Order, before becoming Secretary of State for Air in David Lloyd George's Coalition Liberal Party. After the coalition lost power, and Guest was unseated, he rejoined the Conservatives, winning Drake and holding it until he died. He was succeeded by his brother, Henry, a Liberal.

THURSDAY 15th JUNE 1848

Plympton Railway Station was opened, as part of the South Devon Railway, which had purchased the branch line from the Plymouth and Dartmoor Railway, a horse-drawn operation. From 1904, Plympton was the eastern terminus for suburban services, which saw 'steam railmotors' brought in to combat the threat posed by electric trams. It closed to passengers in 1959.

THURSDAY 16th JUNE 1836

'The father of the British Navy' Admiral Sir Edmund Robert Fremantle, commander-in-chief, Devonport, 1896 to 1899, was born. A career naval officer, the son of a vice-admiral, he served his country for 52 years after entering the Senior Service in 1849, aged 13. Career highlights included commanding HMS *Dreadnought*. Upon becoming commander-in-chief, Plymouth, he was promoted to Admiral later that year, and he retired in 1901, aged 65.

MONDAY 17th JUNE 1940

The old Regent Cinema in Frankfort Gate reopened as the 'Odeon Cinema', having been transformed by German Oscar Deutsch who was responsible for establishing the Odeon brand, and its art deco look, across the country. Legend has it that Deutsch invited Gwyther Prance of the Regent Cinema to lunch, during which he told Prance of his plans to build a new cinema in Plymouth that would put the Regent out of business. The alternative, Deutsch suggested, was for Prance to sell the Regent to him. Deal done. Deutsch died a year later and the Odeon chain was sold to the Rank Organisation.

THURSDAY 18th JUNE 1846

Royal Assent was given to an Act of Parliament approving a cemetery at Ford Park, outside the boundary of the Three Towns. The cemetery was needed to alleviate overcrowding in the churchyards of the local parish churches and was opened, under the auspices of the Plymouth, Stonehouse & Devonport Cemetery Company, in 1848. The timing of its opening was gloomily appropriate as Plymouth was just about to be the epicentre of one of the worst outbreaks of cholera in the country. More than 400 burials took place at Ford Park in its first year. It is reckoned that a quarter of a million people have since been buried within its grounds.

TUESDAY 19th JUNE 1945

The Royal Mail Line's ship *Drina* disgorged the first liner passengers to land at Plymouth since 1940. She arrived after a 16-day voyage from Argentina, carrying 25 passengers and 7,000 tons of meat destined for British troops in Germany. The meat, that is, not the passengers.

FRIDAY 20th JUNE 1947

'The Devon Belle', a luxury express passenger train, pulled out of London's Waterloo Station for the first time. The Devon Belle was Southern Railway's way of signalling an end to the austerity of the World War II years. It was made up entirely of Pullman coaches, on which all seats were available for reservation, and included an observation carriage at the rear of the train. The Devon Belle left Waterloo at noon, with the first passenger stop at Sidmouth some three-and-a-quarter hours later. The train divided at Exeter, with the back going on to Ilfracombe and the front to Plymouth's Devonport, Devonport Junction, North Road and Friary Stations, arriving at the final destination after a journey of about five-and-a-half hours. Early popularity did not sustain, however, and the Plymouth service was abandoned in 1949. By 1954, the bell had tolled altogether for the Devon Belle.

SUNDAY 21st JUNE 1840

Edward Gibbons was born at his father William's chemist shop in Treville Street. Coincidentally, for one whose name was to become synonymous with stamp-collecting, he came into the world in the same year that Britain issued the Penny Black, the world's first postage stamp. Although 'Stanley', as he was known, worked for his dad after the death of his eldest brother, William, Gibbons encouraged his son's hobby by allowing him to set up a counter in the chemist's, and Edward began developing his stamp business. He was helped by the purchase, from two sailors, of a sackful of rare Cape of Good Hope triangular stamps. After his father's death, Edward moved to London to expand further, and Stanley Gibbons & Co., publishers of the now internationally famous Stanley Gibbons stamp catalogue and other stamp-related books and magazines, was set up. In the year ended 31st December 2011, it had total sales of more than £35.7m and a profit before tax of more than £5.1m. Proof that philately will get you somewhere.

THURSDAY 22nd JUNE 1911

Millbay Park was officially opened as a recreation ground by Deputy Mayor John Winnicott in the city's celebrations for the coronation of King George V, at which Mayor Henry Hurrell was representing the city. The park, situated at the junction of West Hoe Road and Citadel Road, Plymouth, was a military barracks during the 18th and 19th centuries and hosted French, Spanish and Russian prisoners of war.

WEDNESDAY 23rd JUNE 2004

Season-ticket sales for Home Park topped the 10,000 mark for the first time in Plymouth Argyle's history as the Green Army relished the prospect of Championship football in the city for the first time.

SATURDAY 24th JUNE 1775

English clergyman and writer of hymns, John Kempthorne was born in Plymouth Dock, the son of Admiral James Kempthorne, and baptised two months later in Stoke Damerel. He was educated at St John's College, Cambridge, and subsequently became a Fellow there. After taking Holy Orders, he rose to become a Prebendary in Lichfield Cathedral from 1826. He is sometimes credited with writing the hymn 'Praise the Lord! Ye Heavens Adore Him', still sung regularly in churches today.

MONDAY 25th JUNE 1860

Canon William Vaughan, the second Roman Catholic bishop of Plymouth, laid the foundation-stone at the Church of St Michael and St Joseph in Prince's Gardens at Mutton Cove. The church was intended to be for the Catholics in Devonport and the sailors who were regularly in port, and was built on land provided by the Secretary of State for War, Lord Panmure. It became the military chaplaincy for the army and navy, as well as for civilians.

WEDNESDAY 26th JUNE 1907

Alexandra Park, in Keyham, was officially opened. The park, off Royal Navy Avenue, on the brow of the hill between Keyham and Keyham Barton, provides panoramic views over the River Tamar and the Dockyard. During World War II, it was used as a barrage-balloon station.

WEDNESDAY 27th JUNE 1962

Plymouth College-educated singer and actor Michael Ball was born. Ball, best known for the song 'Love Changes Everything' and musical theatre roles such as Edna Turnblad in *Hairspray* – for which he won the 2008 Laurence Olivier Award for best actor in a musical – was born in Bromsgrove, but his family moved to Dartmoor when he was three years old. When he was 11 he became a boarder at the college, where he spent four years.

FRIDAY 28th JUNE 1974

The Tour de France made its first visit to England when the 61st running of the race held its second stage – a circuit stage – on the A38 Plympton bypass. The stage was won by Dutch rider Henk Poppe, and was the only stage of any Tour de France that he won. The Tour itself was won by Belgian Eddy Merckx, the best rider the world has ever seen, and was the last of his five successive Tour victories.

SUNDAY 29th JUNE 2008

A bronze name-plaque from the Royal Navy war memorial on Plymouth Hoe was stolen, with shameless thieves returning the following night to purloin three more. Two of the plaques were later sold for scrap, raising only a few hundred pounds, but were recovered – two were damaged beyond repair. The cost to reinstate them was more than £17,000. The Commonwealth War Graves Commission replaced the stolen plaques, which list the names of some 23,000 people who died for their country.

SATURDAY 30th JUNE 1888

The headquarters of the Marine Biological Association was opened by Professor William Flower, director of the Natural History Museum and president of the Zoological Society, at Citadel Hill. The MBA chose the site under the Royal Citadel offered by the War Department for its laboratory and aquarium because it gave them direct salt-water contact, and a variety of species of both animals and plants. The ceremony was also attended by Sir James Clarke Lawrence, the Prime Warden of the Fishmongers' Company which, despite its vaguely Monty Pythonesque overtones, is actually one of the Great Twelve City Livery Companies.

TUESDAY 30th JUNE 1992

Dr David Owen became Baron Owen, of the City of Plymouth, following his elevation to the peerage. Lord Owen elected to sit in the House of Lords as a crossbencher. A former Labour Foreign Secretary and ex-leader of the Social Democratic Party, some people – notably Margaret Thatcher – expressed the opinion that his natural home was the Conservative Party. Three Conservative ministers of state under John Major's Premiership have claimed that Major was ready to offer Owen a cabinet post but backed away after resignation threats from colleagues. Owen, himself, often stated that he would never join the Conservatives.

JULY

SUNDAY 1st JULY 1906

Twenty-eight people died when a boat train from Plymouth to London Waterloo crashed. The London and South Western Railway steam locomotive failed to take a very sharp curve at the eastern end of Salisbury railway station, derailed, and collided with a milk train and a light engine. Claims that the driver, who had the train taking the strain at 70mph in a 30mph zone, had been bribed to go fast by rich New Yorkers who had docked at Plymouth before boarding the locomotive, were dismissed. A more plausible explanation was that the driver, who was taking a non-stopping train through Salisbury for the first time, did not appreciate the risk of high speeds there.

WEDNESDAY 2nd JULY 1578

The friendship of Francis Drake and Thomas Doughty ended in somewhat spectacular fashion when the former had the latter beheaded. The two, along with John Wynyer, had set sail from Plymouth for what would become Drake's celebrated circumnavigation of the globe, but fell out when the aristocratic Doughty's ship, the Swan, became separated from the rest of the fleet during a storm. Obviously, Drake was convinced that Doughty was practising witchcraft and had him tried for mutiny, treason and witchcraft. The execution set an important precedent; that a ship's captain is its absolute ruler, regardless of the rank or social class of its passengers. Before his fate, Doughty had requested that he and Drake receive Communion together. "And after this holy repast," wrote Francis Fletcher, "they dined also at the same table together, as cheerfully, in sobriety, as ever in their lives they had done aforetime, each cheering up the other, and taking their leave, by drinking each to other, as if some journey only had been in hand."

THURSDAY 2nd JULY 2009

Some cities have all the luck – mod-turned-crooner Rod Stewart rocked Home Park with a storming two-hour-plus set that included all the favourites, including community-sing-a-long versions of 'Maggie May' and 'Sailing'. Appropriately enough, given the venue, Rod celebrated singing 'Hot Legs' by booting signed footballs into the crowd, displaying all the skills that once saw him given an apprenticeship at Brentford Football Club before the bright lights of rock 'n' roll crooked its finger and Griffin Park's loss became music's gain.

SATURDAY 2nd JULY 1938

Politician David Owen, Foreign Secretary between 1977 and 1979 and leader of the short-lived Social Democratic Party between 1983 and 1990, was born in Plympton. A Doctor of Medicine, Owen was elected Labour Member of Parliament for Plymouth Sutton in 1966, and, eight years later, he narrowly won next-door Plymouth Devonport from Conservative incumbent Dame Joan Vickers. He held it in the 1979 General Election by 1,001 votes and drew from a well of personal support, after leaving the Labour Party to form the SDP, to make Devonport a safe seat until he was elevated to the peerage in 1992. As a Labour MP, he was Minister of Health before becoming, at the age of 38, the youngest Foreign Secretary since Anthony Eden 40 years earlier. He resigned from the Labour Party after fellow Plymothian Michael Foot became leader in 1980, and formed the SDP with former Labour politicians Roy Jenkins, Bill Rodgers and Shirley Williams. Nine years later, after the SDP formed an electoral alliance with the Liberal Party which briefly threatened to take power from the unpopular pre-Falkland War Conservative government, Owen wound up the party when its members decided to formally merge with the Liberals. He served the remainder of his term as an independent MP until the 1992 General Election.

WEDNESDAY 3rd JULY 1940

The Royal Navy seized the French personnel carrier *Le Poulmic* at Plymouth after the surrender of the French forces to the Nazis. *Le Poulmic*, an old French trawler, was used by the Navy as a minesweeper and general workboat, carrying out duties in and around the Plymouth area. But not for long – see 6th October.

MONDAY 4th JULY 1569

Sir Francis Drake married Saltash maid Mary Newman in St Budeaux Church, Plymouth, having already sailed to the Spanish Main. Sir Francis, perhaps the most famous Plymothian of all, was not born in the city, but 20 miles away in Tavistock sometime in 1540 (possibly – the date has been calculated from portraits of the privateer, navigator, slaver, pirate and politician). Eight years after the couple's nuptials, he set sail for his round-the-world swashbuckle, arriving home just in time for his 12-year marriage to come to an end with Mary's sudden demise. Drake was later married for the second time, to Elizabeth Sydenham.

SATURDAY 4th JULY 1908

Plymouth's first Boy Scout troop was established as Lieutenant-General Robert Baden-Powell's book, *Scouting For Boys*, took as grip on the imagination of the country's young males. Based at All Saints' Church in Harwell Street, the 1st Plymouth was one of the first troops in the country to ride the crest of the new wave. Baden-Powell was a hero to schoolboys after his Boer War exploits so when he rewrote his books for soldiers on military reconnaissance to aim them at a younger market, he was always likely to be on a winner. The camp-fire camaraderie proved to be a big hit, prompting no lesser person than King Edward VII to suggest Baden-Powell should resign from the Army as he could better serve his country by promoting the Scouting movement. Soon after making the move, Baden-Powell was in Plymouth to inspect some 300 scouts, all of whom no doubt promised to do their duty to God and the King – to help other people at all times, and to obey the scout law.

SUNDAY 5th JULY 1992

Former Royal Air Force station and flying-boat base RAF Mount Batten was closed, with the land and buildings being handed over to the Plymouth Development Corporation.

TUESDAY 5th JULY 2005

Nigerian international centre-back Taribo West joined Plymouth Argyle, arriving at Home Park by way of both Milan clubs, Kaiserslautern, Partizan Belgrade and Derby County, after competing in two World Cups, and winning an Olympic gold and a Uefa Cup-winners' medal. West spent a disappointing three months at Home Park, playing just five times.

SATURDAY 6th JULY 1940

Plymouth suffered its first air-raid of World War II. Three Luftwaffe bombs were launched on the Swilly Corporation housing estate in the late morning, killing three people and injuring another six. According to Commonwealth War Graves Commission papers, the first Plymothians to become casualties of the war in their own city were 33-year-old Blanche Margaret Ellnor and Harry Swinburne, 58. Their homes and six other houses, 132-146 Swilly Road, were hit, the blasts flattening three and rendering two others irreparable.

THURSDAY 7th JULY 1988

The Plymouth Falklands Maritime Memorial was dedicated by Lord Mayor of Plymouth Gordon Draper in the garden of remembrance in the old Bull Ring on Plymouth Hoe. The memorial is dedicated to: 'The members of the Royal Navy, Royal Marines, Royal Fleet Auxiliary and Merchant Navy whose names are recorded here. They gave their lives in the service of this country and for the defence of freedom in the Falkland Islands and the South Atlantic 1982.' It lists 131 names and the ships on which they served: HMS *Ardent,* HMS *Antelope,* HMS *Argonaut,* HMS *Fearless,* HMS *Coventry,* HMS *Glamorgan,* HMS *Hermes,* HMS *Invincible,* HMS *Sheffield*; the Royal Fleet Auxiliaries *Fort Grange, Sir Galahad,* and *Sir Tristram*; and the merchant ship *Atlantic Conveyor.*

TUESDAY 7th JULY 1959

Work began on the Tamar Road Bridge by the Cleveland Bridge & Engineering Company, who had submitted the lowest tender for the work – £1.35m. Before the bridge's construction, the lowest road crossing of the River Tamar was Gunnislake New Bridge, ten miles north of the city – a single-lane structure. When the Tamar Bridge was built, it was the longest suspension bridge in the country with a central span that measured 1,100ft.

SATURDAY 8th JULY 1797

News reached the world of the death of three Royal Marines by the names of Lee, Coffy, and Branning who were executed by firing squad on Plymouth Hoe, having previously been found guilty of attempting to stir up a mutiny at Stonehouse Barracks. A crowd of 30,000 people were warmed up for the execution by the public flogging of another marine – who was taken back to barracks after receiving 500 of 1,000 prescribed lashes – before the main event. According to a contemporary report in the *Sherborne & Yeovil Mercury*, the three marines 'knelt on their coffins for a few minutes, when an officer of marines came and drew the caps over their faces, and a party of 20 marines immediately came down and put a period to their existence by discharging the contents of their muskets through their bodies... the whole forming, perhaps, one of the most awful scenes that the human eye ever witnessed'. It was Plymouth's final public execution. For the time being, at least.

TUESDAY 9th JULY 1872

George Wightwick, the first architectural journalist, died. Wightwick, a Welshman, moved to Plymouth to first, work with and, then, succeed John Foulston. Like his mentor, he became well-known in Plymouth as an architect, as well as an actor and comedian. He designed, among other buildings, the Plymouth Mechanics' Institute in Princess Square, the Post Office at Devonport, the Devon and Cornwall Female Orphan Asylum in Lockyer Street, and Athenaeum Terrace.

SATURDAY 10th JULY 1943

The body of Polish Prime Minister-in-exile General Wladyslaw Sikorski was brought ashore from the destroyer *Orkan* at Plymouth Dockyard on its way to London. The commander-in-chief of the Polish Armed Forces had been killed six days earlier when his plane crashed into the sea 16 seconds after take-off from Gibraltar Airport.

THURSDAY 11th JULY 1907

Efford Cemetery was opened by Mayor of Plymouth John Winnicott. A crematorium was added in 1934. The cemetery's most solemn days came in March and April 1941, when it staged mass burials for Plymothians killed in Luftwaffe blitzes on the city. In front of graves draped with the Union Flag, a service was attended by the Bishop and Roman Catholic Bishop of Plymouth and officers from the Army, the Royal Air Force and the Royal Navy. A communal grave at Efford contains 397 Plymouth civilians killed in the air-raids and there is a monument to them and to all civilian casualties of the war.

SATURDAY 12th JULY 1834

Captain John Pilfold, a Royal Navy officer who fought during the French Revolutionary and Napoleonic Wars, died. Pilford was most noted for his skilful command of HMS *Ajax* in Nelson's division at the Battle of Trafalgar whilst only a lieutenant (he was given charge after his captain had been called to give evidence in a court martial against a fellow captain) for which he was honoured with the Trafalgar medal. He died in 1834, having retired to, among other things, fund the lifestyle of his nephew, the poet Percy Bysshe Shelley, after a debilitating stroke. He was buried at St George's Church, Plymouth, which was destroyed in World War II. The graveyard became a car park.

FRIDAY 12th JULY 1776

Captain James Cook, arguably Britain's greatest maritime explorer, embarked from Plymouth in search of the Northwest Passage from the Pacific Ocean to the Atlantic. Cook and his men sailed HMS *Resolution* and HMS *Discovery* around the Cape of Good Hope to reach the west coast of America in February 1778. They continued north but failed in an attempt to pass through the Arctic Ocean during the summer months. Cook put down in Hawaii to prepare for another try the following season but, soon after sailing for the attempt, storm damage to the *Resolution* obliged them to return to Kealakekua Bay for repairs. Relations with the natives had become tense and the theft of a ship's cutter led to a dispute which ended with Cook being stabbed to death by a chief named Kalanimanokahoowaha. That's easy for you to say.

MONDAY 13th JULY 1772

Nearly four years before setting off in search of the Northwest Passage, James Cook had embarked from Plymouth in a Royal Society-commissioned search of a mythical Great Southern Continent, Terra Australis. This time, he was more successful (obviously, since he returned in one piece). His ship HMS *Resolution*, accompanied by HMS *Adventure*, sailed around the Cape of Good Hope, but soon became icebound and he was unable to reach Antarctica. Although he did not see it, Cook charted enough of the South Pacific to show that it would have to be a frigid wasteland and, therefore, not an economically productive addition to the British Empire. During the voyage, Cook determined the location of many new South Pacific islands with incredible accuracy thanks to a new and highly accurate clock, the Larcum Kendall K1 chronometer. He also surveyed, mapped and took possession for Britain of South Georgia. Surely nothing bad could come of that?

MONDAY 14th JULY 1941

The Prime Minister of New Zealand, Peter Fraser, visited Plymouth to show support for its people after the Luftwaffe's pounding of the city. Such visits from Commonwealth dignitaries, as well as British royalty and high-ranking politicians, were not unknown during the conflict. Only two days before Fraser's trip, Vincent Massey, the High Commissioner of Canada, had been in town.

SATURDAY 14th JULY 1827

James Rendel's Laira Bridge, which cost £27,126, was opened by the Duchess of Clarence. With the exception of the River Thames' Southwark Bridge, it was the largest iron structure then existing, and the achievement earned Rendel a Telford Medal, the highest prize awarded by the British Institution of Civil Engineers. Four years later, Rendel introduced a new system of crossing rivers by means of chain ferries worked by steam. Floating bridges based on this principle were put up at Torpoint and Saltash across the Tamar, bridging the divide between Devon and Cornwall and earning him a second Telford medal.

WEDNESDAY 15th JULY 1931

The official opening ceremony for Roborough Airport was performed by the Prince of Wales – somewhat oddly, in the Council Chamber in Plymouth city centre. The future Edward VIII, who had been unable to fly into the aerodrome he was opening because of bad weather, was presented with a silver model of his Moth aeroplane to mark the occasion. The airport closed on December 23rd, 2011.

TUESDAY 16th JULY 1723

Sir Joshua Reynolds, a founder and first president of the Royal Academy, was born in Plympton. Reynolds was an apprentice to portrait painter Thomas Hudson before an Italian sojourn, when he studied the Old Masters and acquired a taste for the 'Grand Style'. Returning to live in London, he was befriended by the good and the great, including Dr Samuel Johnson, Oliver Goldsmith, David Garrick and fellow artist Angelica Kauffmann. In 1768, he became the Royal Academy's inaugural president and, the following year, he was knighted by George III. On becoming Mayor of Plympton in 1772, he told the king that the appointment gave him more pleasure than any other he had received apart from those which the king had bestowed. Creep. Reynolds painted 3,000 portraits before losing the sight of his left eye, which finally forced him into retirement. He often claimed that he "hated nobody", and William Makepeace Thackeray believed "of all the polite men of that age, Joshua Reynolds was the finest gentleman". Maybe not a creep, then. Thomas Bernard, later Bishop of Killaloe, wrote in his verses on Reynolds: "Dear knight of Plympton, teach me how/To suffer, with unruffled brow/And smile serene, like thine/The jest uncouth or truth severe..."

MONDAY 16th JULY 1962

Plymouth Library acquired an instant 'naval studies' section when commander-in-chief, Plymouth, Admiral Sir Charles Madden, officially presented 15,000 naval books to the city. Sir Charles had not been cleaning out his garage – the books were a donation from the Royal Naval Port Library and Plymouth Command Officers' Library, to be known as 'The Mount Wise Collection'. The Port Library had been a part of the Plymouth Naval War College, which had closed at the end of World War I. A section of the building was retained for the library, however, but their relative lack of use persuaded the Navy that their books would be better off where a wider audience could use them.

SATURDAY 17th JULY 1948

Diminutive dancer, director and choreographer Wayne Sleep was born in Plymouth. The two things that he is famous for that everyone knows are that: (a) at 5ft 2in tall in his ballet shoes, Wayne is the shortest male dancer ever admitted into the Royal Ballet School and would not have gained a place had he not left his entrance audition early and missed his final physical examination; and (b) in 1973, on BBC TV's *Record Breakers*, he set a world record by doing an entrechat-douze – a jump with 12 foot-beats, a feat of the feet which still stood at the time of going to press.

FRIDAY 17th JULY 1970

Speedway's on-off relationship with Pennycross Stadium came to an end with Plymouth Devils' last race there. The stadium had witnessed two deaths in its 40-year flirtation with the two-wheeled sport – Australian rider Noel Johnson, in 1931, and Dick Jenkins, 20 years later, on his debut appearance at the track.

FRIDAY 18th JULY 1952

The Navy, Army and Air Force Institute Club was opened in Notte Street by Princess Margaret on her first official visit to the city. It had a tavern, dance hall, restaurant and kitchen on the ground floor; reading room, games room, lounge and seven bedrooms for members of the Women's Royal Naval Service on the first floor; and 42 double rooms on the second floor for male service personnel.

WEDNESDAY 18th JULY 1666

The foundation-stone of the Royal Citadel was laid by the Earl of Bath John Granville. The Citadel was designed by the Crown's Surveyor-General of Ordinance Sir Bernard de Gomme on the orders of King Charles II, who realised the importance of Plymouth as a channel port during the Dutch Wars of 1664 to 1667. Possibly because of Plymouth's support for the Parliamentarians in the Civil War, its guns could also fire on the town and De Gomme faced some criticism over his unorthodox design: for instance, when Samuel Pepys visited in 1683, he wrote that "De Gomme hath built very sillily". The Citadel was the most important English defence for more than 100 years and was regularly strengthened. It is still used today by the military, but it is also a tourist attraction.

FRIDAY 19th JULY 1588

The Spanish Armada, led by the Duke of Medina Sidonia, appeared off St Michael's Mount in Cornwall. The English fleet was trapped in Plymouth Harbour by the tide and the Spanish proposed to sail into the harbour, incapacitate the defending ships at anchor, and go on to attack England and overthrow Elizabeth I. However, the Duke was unable to carry out the proposal because Philip II explicitly forbade it, and opted to sail on towards the Isle of Wight. Soon afterwards, 55 English ships set out from Plymouth to confront them, under the command of Lord Howard of Effingham with Sir Francis Drake as Vice-Admiral. With the help of some severe storms, they succeeded in preventing the Armada from reaching Flanders to transport the famous Tercios de Flandes, a ground force of over 30,000 men led by the Duke of Parma, across the Channel. The boost to England's pride and Elizabeth's standing lasted for some time, and gave heart to the Protestant cause across Europe. The belief that God was behind the Protestant cause was shown by the striking of commemorative medals that bore the inscription: 'He blew with His winds, and they were scattered'.

THURSDAY 19th JULY 1888

The foundation stone of the National Armada Memorial was laid on Plymouth Hoe by Mayor Henry Waring, 300 years to the day that the Spanish raiding party had been sighted from the same spot.

MONDAY 20th JULY 1959

HMS *Plymouth*, built – where else? – at Devonport Dockyard, was launched by Viscountess Astor. *Plymouth*, a Rothesay class frigate, served in the Royal Navy from 1959 to 1988. She was one of the first Royal Navy ships to arrive in the South Atlantic following the 1982 Argentine invasion of the Falkland Islands. She was attacked by five Argentine Dagger aircraft and damaged: one bomb hit the flight deck, detonating a depth charge and starting a fire; one went straight through her funnel; and two more destroyed her Limbo anti-submarine mortar. None exploded and she survived to rejoin the task force. Alongside HMS *Antrim*, HMS *Brilliant* and HMS *Endurance*, she helped recapture South Georgia during Operation Paraquet. *Plymouth* landed Royal Marines from her Westland Wasp helicopters and bombarded Argentine troop positions on the island with her guns.

TUESDAY 21st JULY 2009

Plymouth diver Tom Daley struck gold in the FINA World Championships in Rome. Daley, 15, surprisingly won the individual 10m platform title despite his dive boasting a lower tariff than his two nearest opponents, Qiu Bo and Zhou Luxin, who both performed poorly. The young Plymothian received four perfect 10s from the judges on his final dive.

THURSDAY 22nd JULY 1937

Doctor Who actress Adrienne Hill was born in Plymouth. She appeared in the BBC science fiction television series in the mid 1960s as Katarina, a companion of the Doctor, played by William Hartnell. She was in only five episodes of two storylines – *The Myth Makers* and *The Daleks' Master Plan* – and was one of the few of the Doctor's companions to be killed.

FRIDAY 22nd JULY 1988

The 27ft-high stainless steel sundial, on the intersection of Armada Way and New George Street, was unveiled by Her Majesty the Queen. It is set in a pool of continuously pouring water, ringed by granite and metal seats highlighting countries of the world, and cost £70,000. It was designed by architect Carole Vincent, from Boscastle, in Cornwall, and runs around 17 minutes behind Greenwich Mean Time. Which is not, apparently, an excuse to be late for work.

WEDNESDAY 23rd JULY 1746

Plymouth Member of Parliament and Mayor Sir Frederick Leman Rogers was born. Born in to it, in fact. His uncle John and grandfather Sir John were also mayors, while great-grandfather John was MP between 1713 and 1721. Sir Frederick became Plymouth Mayor in 1774-75, and was MP from 1780 to 1784 and again from 1790 to 1797, when he died.

TUESDAY 23rd JULY 2002

Her Majesty the Queen presented the Royal Navy with a new Colour on the flight deck of the Navy's largest vessel, helicopter carrier HMS *Ocean*. It was only the third time in the Navy's history that the monarch had presented the Colour, a 3ft 8in by 3ft silk flag bearing a crown and Royal Cypher. The ceremony took place in Plymouth Sound in front of the ship's company. Earlier, the lifeboat *Sybil Mullen Glover* was officially christened by the Queen at Queen Anne's Battery Marina. The new Severn class lifeboat was named after a local artist who had died seven years previously and left nearly half of the £2m cost of the vessel as a legacy.

WEDNESDAY 24th JULY 1889

Turnchapel Pier was formally opened and a regatta held afterwards. The pier, which was 60 yards long and three yards wide and had a waiting-room at the end, was built for steamers going to and coming from Plymouth. It was demolished in 1956.

MONDAY 25th JULY 1440

King Henry VI granted a Royal Charter to the Mayor of Plymouth and Commonality for fairs, feasts and markets. Plymouth was the second municipal borough in the country, after Kingston-upon-Hull, but the first to be granted by an Act of Parliament, a status it maintained until the passing of the Municipal Corporations Act of 1835.

FRIDAY 25th JULY 1851

George Errington was consecrated first Roman Catholic Bishop of Plymouth, a post he held until March 1855. The following year, he founded St Boniface's Catholic College, where, in 1995, he had a House named after him.

THURSDAY 26th JULY 1962

The Queen formally opened the Civic Centre – the Council House and Municipal Offices – in Armada Way. The 14-storey building cost £1.6m, a quarter of which had come from compensation for the battering the city took during World War II. It meant that the city's various administrative departments were all under the same roof for the first time.

SATURDAY 26th JULY 1980

Plymouth-born swimmer Sharron Davies won silver for Great Britain at the Moscow Olympics. Davies had been a household name for four years since she had represented her country as a 13-year-old in the Montreal Games. Two years later she won two golds, as well as a silver and a bronze, in the 1978 Commonwealth Games in Edmonton. She then took the 400-metre individual medley silver in Moscow, ten-and-a-half seconds behind East German Petra Schneider, who later admitted to having been doped. No kidding.

THURSDAY 27th JULY 1815

Napoleon Bonaparte sailed into Plymouth Sound, though not under his own steam. Napoleon had sought political asylum from British captain Frederick Maitland after losing the Battle of Waterloo, and Maitland had taken him, on board HMS *Bellerophon*, from the port of Rochefort to, initially, Brixham. *Bellerophon* then received orders to proceed to Plymouth Sound, where Admiral Lord Keith was anchored aboard his flagship HMS *Ville de Paris*. Napoleon remained on board *Bellerophon*, which was kept isolated from the hordes of curious, and adoring, sightseers by two guardships. Napoleon usually appeared at about 6pm every day for the benefit of the many boats loaded with sightseers, including artist Charles Lock Eastlake who was able to make sketches for a famous portrait. After a week of this spectacle, Napoleon was hustled into exile.

SUNDAY 28th JULY 1588

Sir Francis Drake sent eight hastily-built fire ships – regular warships filled with pitch, brimstone, gunpowder and tar – into the Spanish Armada, which had dropped anchor at Calais and been involved in a stand-off with the English fleet. The Spanish, expecting the ships to explode, cut anchor and ran. This paved the way for the last, and bloodiest, battle of the conflict off Gravelines the following day.

NEW STREET, FORMERLY GREYFRIARS STREET, ON THE BARBICAN, WAS NEW IN THE LATE 1500S

TUESDAY 29th JULY 1924

Prince George had a busy day. After unveiling the Naval War Memorial on Plymouth Hoe in the morning, he officially opened the Devon and Cornwall (ex-service) Tuberculosis Colony in Efford. 'The Efford Colony', as it was more commonly known, was an open-air hospital for servicemen who had contracted tuberculosis during World War I. It lasted just 11 years until the British Legion pulled its £350-a-year funding. More than 50 children needed alternative accommodation when its doors closed.

WEDNESDAY 29th JULY 1931

Mayor James Clifford Tozer opened Central Park – Plymouth's 'green lung' – to the public at an evening ceremony. Around £130,000 had been spent on the project, which included buying land from Lord St Levan and two local residents.

WEDNESDAY 30th JULY 2008

Children's TV boffin Jon Miller died, aged 87. Best remembered as the academic who answered youngsters' questions on the long-running programme *How!*, he was also a regular on Plymouth-based Westward TV's *Westward Diary*. Then, as obituary lister Gavin Gaughan recalled: "He became involved with Television South West... [and] ...had the bad luck to be on TSW's *The Opening Show* on New Year's Day 1982, a tacky, under-rehearsed event in which host Lennie Bennett declared that TSW would stand for 'Television Simply Wonderful'. The next day headlines in the local press called it 'boring, silly rubbish'."

WEDNESDAY 31st JULY 1901

The trailblazing Discovery Expedition – or, to give it its full title, the British National Antarctic Expedition 1901 to 1904 – got underway under the leadership of Plymouth-born Royal Navy captain Robert Scott. It was the first official British exploration of the Antarctic for a generation and its success launched the careers of many who would become leading figures in the heroic age of Antarctic exploration including; Scott, Ernest Shackleton, Edward Wilson, Frank Wild, Tom Crean, William Lashly and Thomas Hodgson. Hodgson was the biologist aboard the HMS *Discovery* and known by the nickname 'Muggins'. He had worked at the Marine Biological Station in Plymouth, was one of the expedition's oldest members, at 37, and had not even been a first choice – the post of naturalist had previously been offered to William Bruce. Hodgson was appointed curator of the Plymouth Museum on his return.

AUGUST

MONDAY 1st AUGUST 1921

'Plymouth's Super Cinema', the 1,400-seater Savoy Picture House just off Union Street, opened its doors, having closed nine months earlier as plain old St James's Hall. It boasted a full orchestra, and a cafe and tea lounge for theatre goers and non-theatre goers alike. Seats ranged in price from two shillings and four pence for the front circle, to nine pence for the front stalls. In the centre circle, they were one shilling and sixpence, three pence more than the back circle. Children were admitted half-price everywhere until 4pm. Plymothians queued round the corner on opening night to see *The Breed of the Treshams*, an English Civil War drama about the redemption of a soldier of fortune played by John Martin-Harvey, and a short starring Snooky the Chimpanzee called *A Tray Full of Trouble*. The Savoy Picture House was destroyed in World War II.

THURSDAY 2nd AUGUST 1945

United States President Harry S Truman stopped off in Plymouth Sound on his way home from the Potsdam Conference to have lunch with King George VI aboard battleship HMS *Renown*. Truman's meeting with Soviet Union Communist Party general secretary Joseph Stalin and British Prime Ministers Winston Churchill and – after the result of the General Election was known – Clement Attlee, in occupied Germany, decided World War II punishment for Nazi Germany, who had unconditionally surrendered nine weeks earlier. The meeting also saw Japan issued with an ultimatum to surrender or meet 'prompt and utter destruction'. After Prime Minister Kantaro Suzuki's declaration that they would ignore the ultimatum, atomic bombs were dropped on Hiroshima and Nagasaki.

MONDAY 3rd AUGUST 1936

More than 5,000 scouts, rover scouts, girl guides and cubs greeted Chief Scout Lord Robert Baden-Powell at a rally at Plymouth Argyle's Home Park as part of a westcountry jamboree. The scouts marched in formation past Lord Baden-Powell, who took their salute, and the pageant included sea scouts from Dublin, whose leader, reported *The Times* 'Bore the flag of the Irish Free State' and more than 100 foreign scouts including a contingent from San Pedro de Macoris, in the Dominican Republic. Lord Baden-Powell told his young audience that scouting "prepared boys to be good citizens who would stick to their duty to King and country".

TUESDAY 3rd AUGUST 2004

Plym II, the first of the newest generation of Torpoint Ferries was launched at Ferguson Shipbuilders in Glasgow. The total investment in three ferries – *Tamar II* and *Lynher II* were the others – was £18m. They are run by a joint committee involving Plymouth City Council and Cornwall County Council.

FRIDAY 4th AUGUST 1871

The Thunderbolt, one of a host of newspapers to have published the latest news down the years, was first printed. It folded three years later. Other short-lived papers that have urged Plymothians to read all about it include: the *Plymouth Chronicle* (1780-1782); *the Patriot*, or *Palladium of British Liberty* (1820); *the Devonport Standard and Plymouth United Services Gazette* (1835-36); and *the Union, or Three Towns Miscellany* (1852).

MONDAY 5th AUGUST 2002

Prolific, controversial, unfashionable, celebrated, and extraordinary artist Robert Lenkiewicz died of a heart attack, aged 60. Loved by the public, dismissed by the experts, London-born Lenkiewicz arrived in Plymouth via Cornwall – where he made a lifelong acquaintance in Peregrine Eliot, the Earl of St Germans – after local artist John Nash offered him a Barbican studio. As well as producing standard portraits of people (including Michael Foot and Billy Connolly), he both attracted and painted down-and-outs, putting them up in derelict buildings around Plymouth before making them the subjects of an exhibition of portraits entitled 'Vagrancy'. Subsequent projects dealt with other taboo subjects such as 'Mental Handicap' (1976), 'Suicide' (1980), and 'Death' (1982). Lenkiewicz was obsessed with the subject of death. He faked his own to see what it was like to be thought of as having died and, after he actually passed away, the embalmed corpse of a tramp that he had befriended – Edwin McKenzie, nicknamed 'Diogenes' because Lenkiewicz found him living in a barrel – was discovered in a secret drawer in a 'death room'. This room also included the skeleton of Ursula Kemp, a 16th-century midwife who was hanged for witchcraft and nailed into her coffin, and a lampshade he claimed had been brought out of Auschwitz allegedly made from the skins of Jews who died in the Holocaust. Despite painting 10,000 works rated of 'national importance' by the British Museum, he possessed only £12 cash when he died, and owed £2m to various creditors.

SATURDAY 5th AUGUST 1939

The 1,800-seater Forum cinema in Devonport showed its first film, *Honolulu*, starring Robert Young and Eleanor Powell. It became a bingo hall 21 years later.

THURSDAY 6th AUGUST 1835

The foundation-stone of the South Devon and East Cornwall Hospital and Plymouth Public Dispensary was laid by the Reverend John Hatchard, vicar of St Andrew's Church. Despite the grand name, because of its position off Greenbank Road, it was more commonly known as 'Greenbank Hospital'. Following the opening of Derriford Hospital, it was demolished and replaced by a new housing estate.

FRIDAY 7th AUGUST 1657

Admiral Robert Blake, regarded by many as second only to Horatio Nelson as Britain's foremost naval officer, died aboard his flagship, the *George*, within sight of Plymouth. As well as being largely responsible for building the largest navy the country had then ever known – from a few tens of ships to well over 100 – he was first to keep a fleet at sea during winter. He developed techniques to conduct blockades and landings, writing *Fighting Instructions*, a major overhaul of naval tactics. He was also the first to maintain attacks despite fire from shore forts. He defended Taunton and Lyme Regis for the Parliamentarians during the English Civil War and distinguished himself in action in the First Anglo-Dutch War, and the Anglo-Spanish War before his death. He was interred at St Andrew's Church before being removed to Westminster Abbey – although his heart is still thought to be buried under the church.

SATURDAY 8th AUGUST 1355

Edward of Woodstock, the Black Prince, arrived in Plympton to begin preparation for what would become one of the three great victories in the Hundred Years War, the Battle of Poitiers, in central France. The Prince, along with his 12,000 men, defeated the French army of 60,000 men and took prisoner the King of France, John II – 'Jean Le Bon' – and his youngest son, Philippe. They, and many French noblemen, were brought back to Plymouth early in 1357. They moved on to Exeter, where they were entertained by the Mayor of Exeter for three days, and arrived in London in May.

FRIDAY 8th AUGUST 1862

Work started on Derry's Clock, currently to be found behind the
Theatre Royal – but which was once the centre of Plymouth – where
George Street, Union Street and Lockyer Street converged. It was
at this junction that the city's trams and buses terminated so was a
natural meeting place. Hence the local wisdom that: "Marriages
may be made in heaven, but, in Plymouth, they are arranged under
Derry's Clock." Actually, it is not a clock, but a fountain. The local
authority was forbidden by Parliament from building a clock tower
but did have permission for a fountain, so they modified architect
Henry Hall's design, called it 'a fountain' and pressed ahead.

WEDNESDAY 8th AUGUST 2001

Plymouth Argyle unveiled their latest signing; ex-Member of
Parliament for Plymouth Devonport and lifelong Pilgrims fan
Michael Foot. Foot was allocated the squad number 90, and his
registration was officially accepted by the Football League, making
him the first Privy Councillor to be available for selection for the
Greens. The signing was a 90th birthday tribute from the club.

SATURDAY 9th AUGUST 2008

Plymouth was named as the UK's most cost-effective place for undergraduates.
The annual NatWest student living index said the city's combination of low
living costs and part-time work possibilities made it the first choice for the
cash-strapped student. Its research found the average Plymouth student
spent £217 per week on living and housing costs, but managed to offset that
with weekly earnings of £115 from part-time work.

MONDAY 10th AUGUST 1942

Albert Casanova Ballard, known to everyone as 'Archie', died, 19 years after
coming to Plymouth from London and being startled by the poverty of the
city. Little has ever been unearthed about his past, but it seems he was nearly
60 when he arrived in Plymouth, and a man of considerable means. Within
a few years, he had built the Ballard Institute in Millbay Road, a glorified
boys' club, the opening of which was attended by 2,500 guests. Archie, who
was made president of Plymouth Argyle in 1932, celebrated the coronation
of King George VI in May 1937 by presenting each boy with a National
Provincial Bank book for an account already containing £5.

MONDAY 10th AUGUST 1925

The Commodore of the Royal Naval Barracks, Charles Royds, inaugurated the Scott Memorial at Mount Wise Park, Devonport. The heavily-metaphored memorial depicts Courage, supported by Devotion and crowned by Immortality, trampling over Fear, Death and Despair. A line from Tennyson's poem *Ulysses* – 'To strive, to seek, to find, and not to yield' – which was found inscribed on a wooden cross in Antarctica after Scott's ill-fated trek to the South Pole in 1912, is reproduced at the base of the memorial. Bronze medallions hold portraits of Scott and his fellow explorers: Oates, Wilson, Bowers and Evans.

FRIDAY 10th AUGUST 1403

French commander William du Chastel led a raid on Plymouth which caused substantial damage in the north of the town. Plymouth played a role in the many wars between England and France in the Middle Ages; in return, it was attacked by French soldiers on several occasions. The worst assault was headed up by du Chastel, who crossed the Channel, marched into Plymouth and occupied the area around what is now Exeter Street – Breton Side. The French dug in and repelled the English, sailing away again the next day after torching the wooden, thatched-roofed, buildings. Plymouth rebuilt and the French act of aggression eventually led to the Battle of Blackpool Sands, in which du Chastel was killed.

TUESDAY 11th AUGUST 1998

Ooooh! The National Firework Championships were staged in Plymouth for the first time, on Mount Batten Breakwater in the Sound. The winners of the event were Northern Lights, of Trowbridge. Aaaaah! The Championships have been held annually in Plymouth ever since, and attract more than 200,000 spectators.

WEDNESDAY 11th AUGUST 1971

Prime Minister Edward Heath sailed in to Plymouth at 5pm at the helm of his 42-foot yacht *Morning Cloud* to lead the British Admiral's Cup team to victory. Heath claimed victory in the punishing 605-mile long Fastnet Race to cheers from a crowd of onlookers, having raced over five days from Cowes, on the Isle of Wight, to the Fastnet Rock off southern Ireland, and into Plymouth.

SUNDAY 11th AUGUST 1839

Robert Bayly, the owner of the country's first telephone, was born in Brunswick Terrace. Bayly was a Devon councillor who put up Alexander Graham Bell in his Tor Grove House home in Weston Peverel when the inventor of the telephone visited the city to talk about his innovation. While there, Bell set up a line that connected the house to the gardener's cottage to help quell the anxieties of Bayly's wife, who felt nervous living in 'such a lonely place' which was 'deep in the country'. The phone was later donated to the City Museum by Bayly's daughter, later Plymouth's first female councillor.

WEDNESDAY 12th AUGUST 1812

The first stone in the breakwater at Plymouth Sound was deposited. With Napoleonic Wars in the wind, it was constructed to provide safe passage for naval vessels and make Plymouth a safe anchorage for the Channel Fleet. It is effectively a wall a mile long across the Sound consisting of 3,670,444 tons of rough stone and 22,149 cubic yards of masonry on the surface. The huge work was first proposed by Scottish engineer John Rennie in 1806 and it cost an equally massive £1.5m, the equivalent of £74.7m in 21st-century terms. Rennie died in 1821 before the breakwater was finished – it took 30 years to build – so the work was completed by his son, Sir John Rennie, and Joseph Whidbey.

THURSDAY 13th AUGUST 1874

Plymouth Guildhall was opened by the Prince of Wales, later Edward VII, replacing an earlier one at the top of High Street that had served the city since 1800. According to a contemporary report in *The Times*, the interior of the new Great Hall 'is 150 feet long, and has at the west end a spacious orchestra, in which it is intended to place a fine organ. One window is filled with stained glass illustrating the scene of the English captains interrupted in their games of bowls on the Plymouth Hoe by the news of the approach of the Spanish Armada. Other windows are to follow representing scenes in the history of the borough...' Built by John Pethick, later Mayor of Plymouth, it was gutted during World War II, but subsequently lovingly restored by the council.

THURSDAY 14th AUGUST 1873

James Moses, the first Devonport Dockyard worker to be elected to Parliament, and Mayor of Plymouth, was born. After an apprenticeship as a shipbuilder, he entered the Dockyard in 1895 and, from these humble beginnings, rose to become Member of the Executive Committee of the Ship Contractors and Shipwrights' Association. Politically, he joined the Labour Party in 1918 and became active locally. Previously, he had been a Liberal member of Devonport Borough Council in 1911, and of the Council of Greater Plymouth. After switching allegiance, he became an Alderman in 1921 and a Borough Magistrate in 1918, before being elected Mayor in 1926/27. He contested Plymouth Drake in 1923 and 1924, before defeating Arthur Shirley Benn in 1929, after which a petition was presented against him, alleging bribery and corruption on the part of his agent. He was cleared of all charges and awarded £3,000 costs.

MONDAY 15th AUGUST 1803

As a result of a meeting in the Plymouth Guildhall 'to consider on the proper and most effectual means of enrolling themselves as volunteers for the defence of the country against the common enemy', i.e. Napoleon Bonaparte's French, a decision was taken to raise two battalions of infantry under a Colonel-in-Chief, Major-General England. The battalions, which quickly numbered nearly 1,000 men between them, included lieutenant-colonels, majors, captains and lieutenants, as well as regular soldiers.

SUNDAY 15th AUGUST 1875

Anglican clergyman, poet, antiquarian of Cornwall, and reputed eccentric Robert Hawker – often known by his second name, Stephen – died. Hawker is best known as the writer of *The Song Of The Western Men*, which includes the chorus line: "And shall Trelawny die? There's 20,000 Cornish men shall know the reason why," although he published the song anonymously. It was Charles Dickens who blew Hawker's cover in the serial magazine *Household Words*. Hawker was also the innovator of the modern custom of the Harvest Festival, which he started in the Cornish village of Morwenstow when he invited his parishioners to give thanks to God for providing for them. Bread made from the first cut of corn was taken at Communion. Despite his Cornish associations, Hawker had impeccable Plymouth credentials. He was born in the vicarage of Charles Church and buried in Ford Park Cemetery.

MONDAY 15th AUGUST 1949

Turner Prize-winning sculptor Richard Deacon was born. Plymouth College-educated Deacon won the annual award for British visual artists in 1987 for his touring show 'For Those Who Have Eyes'. His works are often constructed from everyday materials such as laminated plywood, and he calls himself a 'fabricator' rather than a sculptor.

WEDNESDAY 16th AUGUST 2006

The world record for the most firework rockets launched in 30 seconds – 56,405 – was set by Plymouth University professor Roy Lowry, who co-ordinated the attempt executed by Fantastic Fireworks on the second day of the tenth National Firework Championships in Plymouth. The verification of the achievement by the *Guinness Book of Records* took two months to come through. The record was subsequently more than doubled by a Philippine company.

MONDAY 17th AUGUST 1789

King George III and his queen, Charlotte of Mecklenburg-Strelitz, paraded through Plymouth and Stonehouse, supported by other members of the Royal Family; the Governor of Plymouth, George Lennox; and 300 people of various rank and importance. They were given three cheers at the Triumphal Arch in Stonehouse (to which they responded with a royal bow) before processing to Devonport where, after being greeted by sundry dignitaries, they boarded the *Impregnable* before disembarking for a dockyard inspection. They then returned to their temporary base at Saltram.

TUESDAY 17th AUGUST 1909

Escapologist Harry Houdini demonstrated his talents during his run at the Palace Theatre of Varieties in Union Street. In front of a large crowd that had assembled outside at Stonehouse, Houdini was cuffed around his hands, elbows and neck before jumping from the Halfpenny Gate Bridge into Stonehouse Creek and disappearing from view. It took him less than a minute to unshackle himself, much shorter than the time for which he had been incarcerated in part of his stage act at the Theatre. There, he had called upon five joiners and mechanics at Devonport Dockyard to construct a box from which he would not be able to escape. They made the box and Houdini was duly nailed inside. Twelve minutes later...

SATURDAY 18th AUGUST 1855

Alfred Wallis, fisherman and artist, was born in Devonport. Wallis's parents were from Penzance in Cornwall but they moved to Devonport to find work. Wallis went to sea as a fisherman when he was nine and, in 1887, he and his wife Susan, and her six children from a previous marriage, moved to St Ives. There, he set up a shop selling marine wares and salvaged goods, and it was only after the death of his wife and on retirement from the sea, when he was 70, that Wallis began to paint. His pictures of boats and harbours, on odd-shaped boards with ordinary ship's paint, were an inspiration to artists seeking a new approach. The directness of his 'primitive' vision, and the object-like quality of his paintings, were highly influential in the development of British Modernism (apparently). Alfred Wallis is now recognised as one of the most original British artists of the 20th century.

SUNDAY 19th AUGUST 1677

King Charles II visited St Andrew's Church and 'touched for the King's Evil'. In the Middle Ages, it was believed that the touch of the sovereign of England or France could cure diseases. From 1633, the Book of Common Prayer of the Anglican Church contained a ceremony for this. Scrofula – tuberculosis of the neck, usually a result of an infection in the lymph nodes – was also known as 'the King's Evil'.

SUNDAY 19th AUGUST 2007

Plymouth Argyle manager Ian Holloway was recovering after being rushed to hospital in 'unbelievable pain' less than two hours before the Pilgrims' match at Home Park the previous afternoon. The 44-year-old was taken from the ground to Derriford Hospital by ambulance at 1.15pm and was told he had a kidney stone. Ollie was hit by the pain when he arrived at Home Park to prepare for the match. "As I was rolling around on the floor in my office, I noticed I need a new carpet and I must paint the skirting boards – that is not Premiership quality!" he later joked. "I stood up and I had all this rubbish over me! So, I said to the chairman that I need new carpets and he said he'd check the budget for me. I can't accept shoddy standards the next time I need to roll around on my floor!" In his absence, assistant boss Tim Breacker oversaw Argyle's 1-1 Football League Championship draw against Ipswich Town.

SUNDAY 20th AUGUST 2000

Plymouth Hoe briefly became the focus of the pop music world with the arrival of Radio 1's 'One Big Sunday' roadshow. Among the guests were Kylie Minogue and Spiller, the performing name of an Italian DJ and singer Sophie Ellis-Bextor, whose club anthem *Groovejet (If This Ain't Love)* was announced to a live audience of thousands and listening millions as the country's number one song. It held off a concerted promotional effort by Spice Girl Victoria Beckham to reach the summit with her Truesteppers' track, *Out Of Your Mind*. Rubbing it in, Ellis-Bextor, who had criticised Beckham's marketing technique as 'underhand', wore a T-shirt with the word 'Peckham' on it.

THURSDAY 21st AUGUST 2008

Top Gear presenter James May and wine connoisseur Oz Clarke called in to Plymouth Gin Distillery for a cocktail while filming their TV series *Oz and James' Big Beer*. The Distillery, just off Southside Street in the Barbican, is on the site of a former Dominican Order monastery built in 1431 and has been in operation since 1793. It produces – have a guess – Plymouth Gin, which, by law, can only be produced in – another guess – Plymouth. However, it is owned, and distributed by the French company Pernod Ricard.

FRIDAY 22nd AUGUST 2008

Plymouth-born British modern pentathlete Heather Fell won the silver medal in the women's individual event at the 2008 Summer Olympics in Beijing. She went into the final event, the 3,000m run, 19 seconds behind leader Lena Schoneborn of Germany. Heather closed the gap by nine seconds in Beijing's 30°C (86°F) heat and 50% humidity, but could get no closer.

SUNDAY 23rd AUGUST 1970

Prog rock supergroup Emerson, Lake and Palmer made their live debut at Plymouth's Guildhall, as a warm-up for the rather more famous Isle of Wight Festival a few days later. They were formed from parts of the Nice (keyboardist Keith Emerson), King Crimson (vocalist and bassist Greg) and Atomic Rooster (drummer Carl Palmer). There had been speculation in the music press that they were also looking to recruit legendary American guitarist Jimi Hendrix. Which would then, presumably, have made them HELP. Or ELPH.

THURSDAY 24th AUGUST 1905

Lawyer and politician Sir Dingle Foot, part of the Foot political dynasty, was born in Plymouth. At the age of 26, he became Liberal Member of Parliament for Dundee and served as Parliamentary Secretary to the Ministry of Economic Warfare in Winston Churchill's wartime coalition before losing his seat in the 1945 General Election. He left the Liberals and joined the Labour Party in 1956, becoming MP for Ipswich between 1957 and 1970 and Solicitor General in Harold Wilson's government. Dingle's most famous brother was Michael Foot and their other siblings were Liberal politician John Foot, and Hugh Foot, British Ambassador to the United Nations, whose son was the campaigning journalist Paul Foot. Dingle died in a Hong Kong hotel in 1978 after choking on a bone in a chicken sandwich.

SUNDAY 25th AUGUST 1918

Robin Hood was born in Plymouth. Alright, not Robin Hood exactly, but the actor who, for certain generations, is Robin Hood. Richard Greene was what used to be known as a matinee idol that appeared in more than 40 films, but is best remembered for his portrayal of the leader of the Merry Men known in the long-running British television series, *The Adventures of Robin Hood*. His father, also called Richard, and his mother, Kathleen, were actors with the Plymouth Repertory Theatre.

THURSDAY 26th AUGUST 1652

The Battle of Plymouth, a naval skirmish in the First Anglo-Dutch War, took place, with the Dutch surprisingly coming out on top. It happened when English General-at-Sea George Ayscue spotted a Dutch fleet commanded by his former friend Vice-Commodore Michiel de Ruyter off Plymouth. The following day, Ayscue tried to attack the Dutch, who were now off Brittany. Despite initially having the wind with him, Ayscue's lack of organisation meant that he ceded that advantage to de Ruyter, and the Dutch quickly surrounded the best English ships. When the slower vessels of the English fleet, comprising hired merchantmen, arrived at the scene of the battle, they showed little appetite for the fight, reducing the effectiveness of the numerical superiority of the English. Ayscue therefore decided to break off and retreated to Plymouth for repairs. De Ruyter followed, hoping for re-engagement, but found Ayscue willing only to get his whole fleet safely into port.

FRIDAY 26th AUGUST 1768

Captain James Cook left Plymouth for his first Pacific voyage at the head of an expedition to observe the transit of Venus – when the planet passes directly between the Sun and Earth – and explore the Pacific Ocean in the *Endeavour*. Nearly a year later, he reached Tahiti where, after recovering part of his equipment that had been stolen by the natives, the transit was observed. He then charted New Zealand and explored and claimed possession of eastern Australia before returning to England in June 1771, by way of New Guinea, Java and the Cape of Good Hope.

TUESDAY 27th AUGUST 1940

The Ford House Public Assistance Institution in Wolseley Road took a bad hit from a Luftwaffe air-raid on a bad night of bombing for Plymouth. Thirteen residents of the former Devonport Workhouse died and many others were injured. On the same night, the Great Western Railway liner tender, the *Sir John Hawkins*, which ferried passengers to and from liners on their way from the USA, was badly damaged. After repair, she was taken over by the Royal Navy.

MONDAY 27th AUGUST 2001

Plymouth Argyle embarked on a one-season club-record run of 19 games without defeat with a 3-2 Bank Holiday victory at Rushden & Diamonds. The win followed three defeats and a draw from their opening four games and it was not until December 22nd, when they visited Scunthorpe United and lost 2-1, that they tasted a league defeat again. Rushden & Diamonds were the only side to score more than once against the Pilgrims during the run and 13 sides did not score at all.

MONDAY 28th AUGUST 1944

Major Glenn Miller and his 52-piece orchestra, the American Band of the Allied Expeditionary Force, played three concerts in Plymouth; at the US Navy field hospital, Manadon, the Odeon cinema, and HMS Drake. Queues at the Odeon began an hour and a half before the 10.15pm performance, to which only military and naval personnel were admitted. Less than four months later, Glenn Miller was flying from Bedfordshire to Paris when his plane disappeared without a trace, since, of aircrew, passengers or plane. Miller's status remains 'missing in action'.

FRIDAY 28th AUGUST 1868

Five 6ft-high tidal waves arrived at Plymouth Sound in 65-minute intervals, having been caused by the eruption of Krakatoa the previous day.

MONDAY 29th AUGUST 1603

Adventurer John Sparke was buried in Plymouth. Sparke was a chronicler of the 'Age of Discovery', and notably reported on Sir John Hawkins' second voyage to the Spanish colonies between 1584 and 1585, when Hawkins sought to profit from selling African slaves to the Spanish settlements of the New World. It led to the permanent establishment of the English slave trade between Africa and the West Indies. Sparke's accounts were full of exciting and fabulous anecdotes, including descriptions of rattlesnakes, unicorn horns, man-eating crocodiles, and Spaniards flayed by Indians. His florid reporting, combined with news of gold, silver, and other valuables that the Hawkins voyage brought home, encouraged more English commercial expeditions to the Spanish colonies. Sparke coined many descriptions still in use. For instance, he observed a crocodile with tears in its eyes, feigning injury to capture its intended victim, and wrote in his book the description like a woman shedding tears to have her own way. On returning, Sparke gave an account of tobacco and potatoes to his friend and fellow explorer Sir Walter Raleigh, who brought back samples on his next voyage and was credited with their discovery. Sparke was also Plymouth's first property developer, building the oldest original street in the city, ironically known as New Street. Formerly Greyfriars Street on the Barbican, it was actually new in the late 1500s.

SUNDAY 30th AUGUST 1942

Wladyslaw Raczkiewicz, President of the Polish government-in-exile, visited Plymouth to meet Polish Navy officers and men who had been taking part in convoy escorts. Raczkiewicz was the internationally recognised Polish head of state until 1945, and the Polish government-in-exile was recognised as the continuum to the Polish government of 1939.

MONDAY 31st AUGUST 1925

Trinity House pilot steamboat *W Woollven* was sunk off Plymouth after being caught in the propellers of the Cunard liner, *Antonia*. The pilot boat was slashed on its port side after going around the stern of the *Antonia* off Rame Head.

SEPTEMBER

MONDAY 1st SEPTEMBER 1941

'The first act in the rebuilding of Plymouth was the decision of the City Council made on the 1st September 1941 – within six months of the destruction of the centre of the city – that a Redevelopment Plan should be prepared. The Plan – *A Plan for Plymouth* – by James Paton Watson, CBE, the City Engineer, and Sir Patrick Abercrombie, the Town Planning Consultant, was completed by September 1943, and the basic principles of the Plan were approved by the Council in August 1944.' – Inscription on a tablet in the lobby of Plymouth Civic Centre.

SATURDAY 1st SEPTEMBER 1951

The new Dingles store on Armada Way opened: 40,000 people went in for a look.

WEDNESDAY 2nd SEPTEMBER 1936

Diplomat Sir Marrack Goulding was born in Plymouth. He entered the British Diplomatic Service in 1959 and held postings in Kuwait, Tripoli and Cairo before serving during the early 1970s as Private Secretary to three Ministers of State for Foreign and Commonwealth Affairs; Joe Godber, Julian Amery and Roy Hattersley. Goulding was appointed ambassador to Angola, Sao Tome and Principe in 1983, and, three years later, was appointed Under-Secretary-General for Special Political Affairs under United Nations Secretary-General Javier Pérez de Cuéllar. In de Cuéllar's successor Boutros Boutros-Ghali's restructuring of the Secretariat in 1992, the title of Goulding's post was changed to Under-Secretary-General for Peacekeeping Operations, and the following year he became Under-Secretary-General for Political Affairs, responsible for preventive diplomacy and peacemaking. By the time his tenure ended in June 1997, he was effectively the second most powerful man in the United Nations after Secretary-General Kofi Annan. He died on July 9th 2010.

WEDNESDAY 3rd SEPTEMBER 1746

John Wesley, the father of Methodism, visited Plymouth Dock for the first time, walking there from Plymouth with local preacher Herbert Jenkins. His initial attempt at preaching, to a crowd of rowdy yardies, was not a great success. However, he returned next day, bolstered by supporters from Plymouth, and gradually won over his audience with a simple message based on the truths of the Bible.

FRIDAY 4th SEPTEMBER 1713

Sir John Rogers was elected Member of Parliament for Plymouth, which he served for ten years. Part of a politically active family of merchants, he was also twice Lord Mayor of Plymouth, in 1722 and 1741.

SATURDAY 4th SEPTEMBER 1779

Colonel William Bastard was gazetted to a baronetcy (but declined to assume the title) after saving the arsenal of Plymouth from the French Fleet. Excited by the sight of their countrymen, French prisoners held at Devonport threatened to get out of hand, so East Devon Militia colonel Bastard raised a force of some 500 local 'fencibles' (soldiers liable for home service only), sent half the force to Plymouth and marched the prisoners from Plymouth to Exeter with the other half. Twenty years later, as colonel of the same regiment, his son John Pollexfen Bastard quelled a riot of workmen to prevent the destruction of the Plymouth docks and dockyards. What a pair of Bastards.

MONDAY 5th SEPTEMBER 1898

The New Palace Theatre of Varieties was opened on Union Street. The opening show comprised, among others: the Levey Sisters, Adele and May Lilian, who sang and danced several Persian and hunting songs; the Six Craggs, a team of acrobats; Walter Stockwell, who was described as 'a character vocalist'; and Walter and Edie Cassons, with their highly amusing musical vaudeville *Honours are Easy*. Admission prices were: stalls, two shillings and sixpence; grand circle, one shilling and sixpence; and gallery, one shilling.

SUNDAY 5th SEPTEMBER 1999

Alan Clark, the Conservative Member of Parliament for Plymouth Sutton between 1974 and 1992, died from a brain tumour which he blamed on excessive mobile phone use. Midway through his tenure, Clark appeared on popular darts entertainment television show *Bullseye*, in disguise, as partner to Geoffrey Pollock, treasurer of Plymouth Conservative Club. With Clark answering the questions and Pollock throwing the arrows, the pair reached the final 'Bully's Prize Board', winning a Bontempi electronic keyboard, a 24-piece cutlery set and a Soda Stream fizzy drinks maker. They elected to gamble that treasure trove for the star prize – a two-berth Elddis Whirlwind caravan – but lost.

FRIDAY 5th SEPTEMBER 1986

The Cornish Emigrants Memorial on the wall of the Fishermen's Shelter, by the side of the Admiral MacBride pub on the Barbican, was unveiled by David Kitto, president of the South Australian Cornish Association. A list of the people who had emigrated from Cornwall, through Plymouth, to form the colony in South Australia was placed in a time-capsule behind the plaque.

WEDNESDAY 6th SEPTEMBER 1620

The *Mayflower*, with 102 Pilgrims and crew aboard, set sail from Plymouth for the New World. The *Mayflower* had been chartered by John Carver, the leader of a separatist group of the Church of England that had fled Nottinghamshire for Holland to escape persecution by English authorities. Finding conditions poor, they decided to emigrate to the English colonies in Virginia. Given their religious beliefs, it was perhaps ironic that the *Mayflower* had previously been used to ship wine.

SUNDAY 6th SEPTEMBER 1964

Time was called at the iconic Harvest Home pub on the junction of Pound Street and Tavistock Road after 134 years of supping.

THURSDAY 7th SEPTEMBER 1893

Isaac Leslie Hore-Belisha was born in Devonport. A Liberal Cabinet Minister, who later crossed the floor of the House to become a Conservative, he was Minister for Transport and Secretary of State for War until he was sacked from the War Office in 1940, the apparent victim of anti-Semitism. As Minister of Transport, he rewrote the *Highway Code* and was responsible for the introduction of two innovations that saw the number of road accidents slashed: the driving test, and the Belisha beacon, which marked public crossings. Being Jewish, Hore-Belisha's desire as Secretary of State for War to introduce conscription was criticised by the Conservatives, who believed that he wanted Britain to wage war against Germany with the sole intention of protecting European Jews. His modernisation reforms of the armed services included sacking three of the Imperial General Staff, which infuriated the military establishment. He was briefly Minister for National Insurance in the Conservative Caretaker government of 1945 before standing as a National Independent. He was defeated in Devonport by Labour candidate Michael Foot.

MONDAY 7th SEPTEMBER 2009

Radio presenter Chris Moyles became the longest-serving breakfast DJ on BBC Radio 1 when he broadcast live from Plymouth. Moyles clocked up 2,073 days in the job, breaking the record set by Tony Blackburn more than 30 years earlier, when he kicked off his UK tour.

MONDAY 7th SEPTEMBER 1959

The Plymouth Pannier Market opened, having been built at a cost of £269,548 from a design by local architects Walls and Pearn. The word pannier derived from the French meaning 'basket' and, to reflect modern trends, 'Pannier' was replaced by 'City'.

MONDAY 7th SEPTEMBER 1964

Devonport Kings Road Railway Station closed after 88 years. Fewer than 15 years earlier, it had hosted 38 trains a day. For the first 14 years of its existence, it was a terminal station, with trains to London departing eastwards, but, from 1890, it became a through station, with trains to London departing westwards.

WEDNESDAY 8th SEPTEMBER 1915

King George V and Queen Mary made a two-day World War I visit to Plymouth, to inspect troops, award medals, tour military and naval hospitals, and visit the dockyard.

SATURDAY 8th SEPTEMBER 1962

The Odeon Cinema closed to make way for the redevelopment of Frankfort Gate. *The Loudest Whisper*, starring Shirley MacLaine and Audrey Hepburn, was the final feature. 'A lie by a spiteful child in school leads to tragedy for the women who teach her, when the malicious gossip spreads like wildfire among the citizens of a small town.' Sounds like a cracker. The Odeon name was transferred to the former Gaumont Cinema in Union Street.

SATURDAY 9th SEPTEMBER 1899

The *Western Evening Herald* launched a *Saturday Football Herald*. Fittingly for a paper following Plymouth Argyle, it was printed on green paper. It ceased publication only during both world wars, and the cricket season, before printing its final edition on Saturday 18th December, 1954.

FRIDAY 10th SEPTEMBER 1926

Beryl Tansley was born in Epsom, Surrey. In 1963, she moved to Plymouth and started dabbling in painting, specifically of Plymouth and its people. Bernard Samuels, of the Plymouth Art Centre, convinced her to have an exhibition and the 1975 show resulted in a cover feature in the *Sunday Times Magazine*, followed by her first exhibition in London at the Portal Gallery where she continued to exhibit until her death. In 1979, a film was made about her for *The South Bank Show*, in which she discussed her work with Melvyn Bragg. In 1995, she was made an OBE. Her contribution to the Queen's Golden Jubilee, 'The Royal Couple', featured in the Golden Jubilee Exhibition at Art London, Chelsea. She died in 2008, possibly the most famous popular artist on the planet. What do you mean, you've never heard of her? Did I mention she had married John Cook in 1946?

SUNDAY 10th SEPTEMBER 2000

Major Sir John Jacob Astor MBE died aged 82. 'Jakie' was a son of Viscount Astor and Lady Astor, both of whom had represented the Plymouth Sutton ward as Member of Parliament. Their youngest, a member of the SAS who had been named after a relative who died on the *Titanic* in 1912, made it a hat-trick in 1951 and served in Parliament for eight years. He will be best remembered for an act of considerable political courage when, first in the Conservative Party's Defence Committee and then on the floor of the House, he called in to question his own Government's actions during the Suez crisis and was one of eight Conservative MPs to abstain on a vote of no confidence.

WEDNESDAY 11th SEPTEMBER 1644

Plymouth refused to surrender to the King during the English Civil War. During the duration of the war, Plymouth was in the hands of Parliament forces, who retained it even at a time when the rest of the Westcountry was possessed by Royalists. King Charles I and Prince Maurice came to Plymouth, lodging at Widey House, before summoning the town's governor, Lord John Robartes, to surrender. Robartes said 'no', precipitating a Royalist council of war at which it was decided to maintain a four-year siege on Plymouth led by Sir Richard Grenville.

SATURDAY 11th SEPTEMBER 1976

A 'Declaration of Cooperation' was signed by Plymouth and the Polish city of Gdynia. The aim of the agreement is to broaden the forms of international co-operation and peaceful coexistence in Europe and tighten the bonds forged during World War II, as well as to exchange experience in the field of urban economy. So, as well as there being a Gdynia Way in Plymouth, there is also a Plymouth Square in Gdynia. Plymouth is also twinned with Brest, in France; Novorossiysk, in Russia; San Sebastian, in Spain; and, naturally, Plymouth, Massachusetts, in the United States of America.

FRIDAY 12th SEPTEMBER 2003

Four protesters climbed down after chaining themselves to the Tamar Bridge. The men, members of Fathers 4 Justice, abandoned their protest after just a few hours, following talks with trained police negotiators. They stated that they were prepared to stay there for a month to raise awareness of what they saw as the unfairness of Family Courts.

THURSDAY 13th SEPTEMBER 1470

The Earl of Warwick, accompanied by the Duke of Clarence and the Earls of Pembroke and Oxford, landed in Plymouth and Dartmouth with 2,000 men to agitate the revolt that caused the temporary restoration of Henry VI to the throne in place of Edward IV. Warwick – Richard Neville – was one of the main protagonists in the Wars of the Roses, being instrumental in the deposition of two kings, which later earned him his epithet of 'Kingmaker'. In effect, with Henry addled by years in hiding or captivity, Warwick effectively ruled in his name.

THURSDAY 13th SEPTEMBER 1945

The Tothill Community Centre was officially opened by Lord Mayor Harry Mason. During World War II, Tothill Park was home to an American anti-aircraft unit protecting two railway bridges that were obvious targets for German bombers. After the conflict, the British War Relief Society of the United States gave a large amount of money to Plymouth in recognition of its hosting of American servicemen, £6,000 of which was used to build the centre.

SUNDAY 14th SEPTEMBER 1800

Reverend Derwent Coleridge, the first principal of what is now the University of St Mark and St John, was born at Keswick, Cumberland. The son of poet Samuel Taylor Coleridge, he was appointed principal of the College of St Mark in Chelsea, which later merged with nearby St John's College – both had been set up to meet an urgent educational need for trained teachers at a time when government made no direct contribution to higher education. The college moved to Plymouth in 1973 – by which time students had long since coined the nickname 'Marjon' – where Coleridge had stayed as a young man. Then, he met Mary Pridham, to whom he proposed on a countryside walk at Greenbank. They married in St Andrew's Church in 1827.

SUNDAY 15th SEPTEMBER 1844

Historian and archivist William Henry Kearley Wright was born in Plymouth. He worked at the Bank of Deposit, which collapsed, and South Devon Railway Company, before the committee of the Free Library of Plymouth freely appointed him as librarian in 1876. He persuaded the authorities to put the statue of Sir Francis Drake on the Hoe and to commemorate the tercentenary of the defeat of the Spanish Armada. A member of the Plymouth Institution, he was an author and editor, publishing, among other works, the *Visitors' Guide to Mount Edgcumbe* and the *Illustrated Hand Book to Plymouth, Devonport and Stonehouse*.

SUNDAY 16th SEPTEMBER 1694

The making of Plymouth – the Royal Navy Dockyard at Devonport – was completed. Five years earlier, Assistant Surveyor of the Navy Edmund Dummer had selected a small inlet off the Hamoaze as the location for a dry dock large enough to hold first-rate ships and made of stone. Previously, the Navy had used timber, which was a fire-risk and high-maintenance. Dummer kept his Account of the Generall Progress and Advancement of his Majestie's New Docks and Yard at Plymouth, which explains the logic of his construction. The valuable historical document contained drafts of plans of the site, the yard, and the dry dock, as well as plans and elevations for the officers' dwelling houses. The motivation for his designs lay in wanting to ensure the dockyard maximised available space and allowed greater workforce mobility. Despite his genius, Dummer died a bankrupt in the Fleet debtors' prison.

TUESDAY 17th SEPTEMBER 1889

Canadian Royal Navy captain Frederick Peters, a World War II recipient of the Victoria Cross, was born. However, just three days after the actions which saw him earn the VC, Peters was killed in Plymouth following an air crash in November 1942. He was in a Sunderland seaplane which crash-landed in fog at the entrance to Devonport Dockyard, killing all five on board. It appears that they all escaped after the plane flipped over but could not be found quickly in the fog and the cold water proved too much for all of them, including Peters, whose body was never found.

MONDAY 18th SEPTEMBER 1939

The first air-sea rescue mission of World War II took place when three Sunderland flying-boats from RAF Mount Batten's 228 Squadron rescued 34 crewmen from the tramp-steam SS *Kensington Court* which had been torpedoed 70 miles off the Isles of Scilly. Flight Lieutenant Thurstan Smith found the steamer sinking by the bows and her crew clinging to a single life-raft. He landed nearby to try and pick up some of the men. A second Sunderland captained by Flight Lieutenant John Barratt then arrived overhead and, after assessing the situation, set off on an anti-submarine patrol of the area while Smith edged as close as he dare to the dangerously overcrowded life-raft. The heavy swell could easily have sent the raft crashing through the Sunderland's hull if it approached too near, so the survivors had to be ferried across, four or five at a time, in the aircraft's two dinghies. With 21 seamen eventually on board and already dangerously overloaded, Smith signalled to Barratt that he was taking off. It was then Barratt's turn to alight and pick up the remaining survivors. Despite their overweight condition, both aircraft flew back to Mount Batten safely. For his brave actions, Barratt was awarded the Distinguished Flying Cross at the first wartime investiture.

WEDNESDAY 19th SEPTEMBER 1923

The Lord Bishop of Bradford, Arthur Perowne, formerly the Vicar of St Andrew's Church in Plymouth, laid the foundation-stone for the rebuilding of Abbey Hall at St Andrew's as a memorial to those who lost their lives in World War I.

FRIDAY 20th SEPTEMBER 1839

Royal Navy officer Sir Thomas Hardy, Flag Captain to Admiral Lord Nelson and commander of HMS *Victory* at the Battle of Trafalgar, died. Hardy, who lived in Durnford Street, rose through the ranks to become a Vice-Admiral, but his naval career is defined by just three words, "Kiss me, Hardy", ascribed to him after Nelson was fatally wounded aboard *Victory* in 1805. It has been suggested that what Nelson actually said was, "Kismet, Hardy" meaning that he was meeting with fate. However, there were many witnesses who saw Hardy kneel beside Nelson and kiss him on the cheek. Whatever Nelson said, they were not his final words. Those came later and were actually; "God and my country."

FRIDAY 20th SEPTEMBER 1946

World War II claimed its last Plymothian, more than a year after the end of the conflict. William Wyatt, 67, of Elliott Road, passed away at Mount Gold Hospital as a result of injuries sustained in an air-raid on English China Clay stables at Prince Rock more than five years earlier.

SUNDAY 21st SEPTEMBER 1890

Oscar-winning film art director and special effects expert James Basevi was born in Plymouth. He shared an Oscar for art direction in 1943 with William Darling for *The Song of Bernadette*. He was also nominated for Oscars for *Wuthering Heights* (1939), *The Westerner* (1940), *The Gang's All Here* (1943) and *The Keys of the Kingdom* (1944).

THURSDAY 22nd SEPTEMBER 1796

HMS *Amphion* blew up in Devonport Dockyard, killing 300 out of the 312 aboard. *Amphion*, a Royal Navy fifth-rate ship, had been repaired and was lying alongside the dockyard jetty prior to sailing the next day. As well as her crew, she had more than 100 relatives and visitors on board. The cause of the disaster was never discovered, but it was thought that the ship's gunner, who may have been drunk, had spilled gunpowder near the fore magazine which had accidentally ignited and set off the magazine. Among the few survivors was her captain Israel Pellew, who went on to command a ship at the Battle of Trafalgar. Pellew was blown into the water from which he was rescued, along with several seamen, a woman, and a child.

SUNDAY 23rd SEPTEMBER 2007

Mayor of Plymouth, Michael Fletcher and British middleweight champion boxer Scott Dann, were among 1,000 locals who attended an event in Devonport Park marking a determination to restore it to past glories. A partnership including the Friends of Devonport Park, the Devonport Regeneration Community Partnership, and Plymouth City Council secured funding from the Heritage Lottery Fund and BIG Lottery Fund to restore the park as 'The People's Park'. The park dates back to the 1850s and is home to many historic monuments, including a memorial to the 2,000 Devonport citizens who died in World War I.

THURSDAY 24th SEPTEMBER 1618

Elizabethan sea dog, privateer, merchant and Mayor of Plymouth, William Parker, died. Parker, a friend of Sir Francis Drake, was the first recorded owner of the 'Merchant's House', the city's finest surviving example of a 17th-century residence just off Notte Street. Before he became mayor in 1601-02, Parker sailed alongside Sir Francis Drake during the raid on Cadiz to singe the King of Spain's beard, and was probably the master of Drake's victualling ship in the fleet against the Spanish Armada, the Mary Rose. After a lifetime plundering places like the West Indies and Honduras on behalf of Elizabeth I, his final adventure was as second-in-command of a fleet voyaging to the East Indies in 1618 under Sir Thomas Dale, who wrote that Parker was by then 'unfit for his work being old and corpulent'. Parker died a few months after this glowing reference.

SUNDAY 25th SEPTEMBER 1864

Harold Roberts, the founder of the Millbay Laundry, Cleaning & Dyeing Company Ltd, was born in his parents' eatery in Bedford Street. Millbay Laundry was centred at Millbay Road and Battery Street, Stonehouse, but had shops and agencies all over Plymouth. Like much of Plymouth, the Stonehouse site was destroyed in the night-time air-raid of April 21st, 1941, although work continued, fulfilling military contracts, in small buildings along Battery Street. The Luftwaffe bombs were also responsible for the death of 76-year-old Roberts, who was so heartbroken by the devastation that he fell seriously ill and never recovered. In 1972, the Millbay Laundry, Cleaning and Dyeing Company Ltd was taken over by Kneel's of Exeter.

TUESDAY 25th SEPTEMBER 1945

The Vicarage Road Army Camp in St Budeaux was decommissioned. A hutted camp overlooking the Royal Albert Bridge, the Vicarage Road camp was used by the United States' army to prepare for the 1944 D-Day landings. It was opened in January of that year and, after a short spell as a records and wages office, it hosted around 60,000 troops on their way to the landing ships moored at Saltash Passage. After the Normandy landings, it was used as a reception centre for returning soldiers.

FRIDAY 26th SEPTEMBER 1823

The horse-drawn Plymouth and Dartmoor Railway was opened, mainly to transport large quantities of granite from the moor's quarries to Plymouth for shipping. The railway was the creation of Sir Thomas Tyrwhitt, the founder of Princetown, and the 25 miles of single track initially ran from Princetown to Sutton Harbour and the Cattewater. Later branches were opened to Cann Quarry and Plympton, followed by the Lee Moor Tramway in 1854. By the 1890s, most of the network had been taken over by the Great Western Railway and replaced by conventional railway.

MONDAY 27th SEPTEMBER 1948

The second section of Royal Parade, from Westwell Street to St Andrew's Cross, including Derry's Cross roundabout, was opened, a year after the first. Lord Mayor Herbert Perry performed the honours by removing 'Road Closed' signs and driving along the road in the official car.

SUNDAY 27th SEPTEMBER 1840

Much of the Devonport Naval Base's heritage was destroyed in 'the Great Fire of 1840', not to mention ships *Talavera*, *Imogene* and *Minden*, and an estimated £80,000 of public property.

FRIDAY 27th SEPTEMBER 1957

Radio and television broadcaster John Inverdale was born in Plymouth. Inverdale, who has covered the Olympic Games, rugby and football World Cups, Wimbledon Championships, Open Golf, and numerous other major sporting events for the BBC, is the son of a Royal Navy dental surgeon Captain John Inverdale, who played rugby union for Devonport Services.

TUESDAY 28th SEPTEMBER 2004

Plymouth Titans Rugby Football League Club was formed at a meeting at Stonehouse Creek. Titans were the South West Rugby League champions in 2008.

SATURDAY 29th SEPTEMBER 1945

Plymouth's final tram ran. At its zenith in the mid-1920s, the Plymouth Corporation system had a maximum of 135 cars on the streets of the city, but buses began to nudge them out from the beginning of the following decade and their demise was almost complete by the outbreak of World War II in 1939. Notwithstanding war damage, the route from Drake's Circus to Peverell continued to run on weekdays only – and was the last street tramway in the west of England – but this was discontinued after the conflict.

SATURDAY 30th SEPTEMBER 1961

Travel from Plymouth Friary railway station to Turnchapel ended with the Plymouth Railways Circle's final run along the London and South Western Railway branch line. The journey from Friary, in Beaumont Street, took in Cattewater Junction, Plymstock Station and Oreston.

OCTOBER

TUESDAY 1st OCTOBER 1878

Once upon a time there was a tavern... The Borough Arms Coffee Tavern, in Bedford Street, was opened. The Tavern was a Plymouth Coffee House Company antidote to the city's pubs, and aimed to provide a meeting place 'equal to, or superior to, in outward attractions and inward comfort, the best and most showy public-houses and beershops'. The Tavern – previously a drapery shop – dispensed 96 gallons of tea, coffee and cocoa on opening night and took more than £10. A little more than 20 years later, during which time it hosted the meeting that established Plymouth Argyle Football Club, the Tavern closed.

SATURDAY 1st OCTOBER 1983

Plymouth Raiders basketball side played their first National League Division 2 game at the Mayflower Centre in Central Park. Merseyside Mustangs were Raiders' first opponents, and duly won the game, but only by an unexpectedly tight score, 76-75. Coach Bob Karruck's side went on to win exactly a quarter of the 24 games in their rookie season.

WEDNESDAY 2nd OCTOBER 1935

Tinside Pool, the unique art deco lido on Plymouth Hoe, was officially opened. It closed in 1992, a faded and abandoned shadow of its former self. However, a strident crusade led to a £3.4m renovation and Grade II Listed Building status, and it re-opened to the public in 2005.

SATURDAY 2nd OCTOBER 1501

Catherine of Aragon arrived at Plymouth on her way to marry Prince Arthur, heir to the throne. After an iffy Channel crossing, she made for St Andrew's Church to offer thanks to God for her safe arrival. Prayers said noblemen of Devon and Cornwall quickly formed an escort to take her to Exeter, where she was to stay.

FRIDAY 3rd OCTOBER 1947

German prisoners of war were sent to Westwell Gardens to search for an unexploded bomb dropped six years earlier. The gardens, previously a cemetery attached to St Andrew's Church, were a city-centre park before World War II and trees from there were included in the design of the post-conflict development of the Great Square outside the Civic Centre.

FRIDAY 3rd OCTOBER 1941

The Right Reverend John Henry Garton, Bishop of Plymouth between 1996 and 2005, was born. After a short service commission in the Royal Tank Regiment, he was ordained in 1969 and began his ministerial career as a Chaplain to the Forces.

FRIDAY 4th OCTOBER 1754

Vice-Admiral William Bligh was baptised at St Andrew's Church. He may have been born in Plymouth, although some claim that happened in St Tudy, Cornwall. Whatever (or wherever), it is Tahiti with which William will be forever linked. It was shortly after leaving the island aboard HMS *Bounty* that some of Bligh's crew, led by Master's Mate Fletcher Christian, mutinied. Bligh and 18 loyalists were set adrift and made a remarkable 47-day 3,618 nautical-mile trip to the nearest European outpost of Timor. Bligh went on to serve under Admiral Nelson at the Battle of Copenhagen, and was later appointed Governor of New South Wales, where he was the victim of another uprising, the Rum Rebellion, which saw him deposed in a coup by the New South Wales military – the only successful armed takeover of government in Australia's history. New South Wales was a penal colony but, besides the convicts, there were large numbers of free men engaged in sheep-ranching, commerce, shipping, and rum distilling and trading. Although the rum traffic was illegal, it was one of the most important industries in the colony. No currency was printed in New South Wales; therefore, rum was used like cash, to buy wool, food, land, and houses and to pay wages. Bligh viewed the rum trade as, not only illegal, but immoral, and he wrote and enforced strict laws to destroy the rum traffic during his first months in office.

THURSDAY 5th OCTOBER 2006

The £200m Drake Circus shopping mall opened its doors to shoppers, offering access to nine major stores and 48 smaller shops. Developers P&O Developments admitted that the eclectic mix of architectural styles in the shadow of the ruined Charles Church was going to be something Plymothians would either love or hate and initial reactions certainly bore that out. It won both the inaugural Carbuncle Cup 'for crimes against architecture', as the worst new building in the country, and the *Retail Week* magazine's 'Shopping Location of the Year' award.

SATURDAY 5th OCTOBER 1850

St Dunstan's Abbey was founded by Lydia Sellon, an Anglican nun who played a part in the 19th century English Catholic Revivalist movement. The daughter of a Royal Navy commander, Sellon committed herself to a life of service in 1848 when she felt compelled to answer an appeal to help the poor in Plymouth and Devonport. She set up a range of institutions including a girls' domestic training school; a boys' night school; facilities for the starving; a home for sailors' orphans; and almshouses. She later formed the Church of England Sisterhood of Mercy of Devonport and Plymouth, or 'The Devonport Society', which worked with the clergy of St Peter's in the cholera epidemics of the 1840s. They set up a temporary wooden hospital, comprising 60 beds, in Five Fields above Stonehouse Lake, later Victoria Park, and petitioned the parish priest, George Prynne, for a morning celebration of the Eucharist to strengthen them for their work. So began the first daily Mass in the Church of England since the Reformation, an innovation which aroused controversy, and even bigotry – a mob pelted Sellon's house, threatening to raze it to the ground. St Dunstan's Abbey was later built on the site of the hospital. The Abbey was closed in 1905 but its name lived on in the form of St Dunstan's Abbey School for Girls, which became part of Plymouth College in 2004.

SUNDAY 5th OCTOBER 1947

Politician Tim Smith was born in Plympton. Former Conservative Member of Parliament Smith can dine out on two stories. In 1977, he won a by-election in Ashfield, Nottinghamshire, in which he was supposed to be election-fodder, overturning a Labour majority of nearly 23,000. He was unable to hold the seat in the subsequent General Election but returned to Parliament in 1982 when he won the safe Tory constituency of Beaconsfield. On the subject of election-fodder, the young Labour candidate who finished a distant third in that poll was Tony Blair.

SUNDAY 6th OCTOBER 1940

The French personnel carrier *Le Poulmic*, which was being used by the Navy as a minesweeper, struck a mine and sank off Penlee Point or, officially, at a bearing '200 degrees and 11 cables from the Breakwater light'. She is now a popular wreck with divers.

TUESDAY 7th OCTOBER 1740

Robert Byng, Member of Parliament for Plymouth from 1728 to 1739 died, aged 36, while in office as Governor of Barbados. Byng, who was also Paymaster of the Navy between 1735 and 1736, was the brother of the unfortunate Admiral John Byng who was shot by a Navy firing squad in 1757 after being court-martialled and found guilty of failing to 'do his utmost' to prevent Minorca falling to the French at the beginning of the Seven Years War.

THURSDAY 8th OCTOBER 1959

Conservative politician Ian Fraser won Plymouth Sutton in the 1959 General Election, following in the Westminster footsteps of Jakie Astor. The modern political landscape of the UK might have been so different had Fraser succeeded in winning the Tory constituency party nomination for which he had first applied. But, he narrowly failed to be selected by Finchley Conservatives, who instead plumped for a 34-year-old Oxford University chemistry graduate called Margaret Thatcher. Fraser was defeated at the 1966 General Election by Labour's David Owen.

SATURDAY 9th OCTOBER 1943

Other Robert Ivor Windsor-Clive became the third Earl of Plymouth, a title which has diddly squat to do with the city. Robert George Windsor-Clive was created first Earl of Plymouth in 1905, after serving as Paymaster General and as first Commissioner of Works from 1902 to 1905, and he passed the title on to his only son, Ivor Miles Windsor-Clive. Ivor's eldest's unusual forename is traditional in the family and derives from a legendary Viking ancestor 'Otho' or 'Othere'. The family seat is Oakly Park, Bromfield near Ludlow, Shropshire.

TUESDAY 9th OCTOBER 1923

Actor Sir Donald Sinden was born in Plymouth. The son of Alfred Sinden and his wife Mabel (née Fuller), he went on to become a star of stage, television and radio across seven decades. He began his career with the Shakespeare Memorial Theatre Company, later joining the Royal Shakespeare Company; enjoyed a prolific film career, starring in *The Cruel Sea*, *Doctor in the House*, and *Doctor at Large*; and was a television leading man in, among other programmes, the sitcom *Never The Twain* and crime drama *Judge John Deed*.

SATURDAY 9th OCTOBER 1886

The Argyle Football Club, forerunners of Plymouth Argyle, played their first game, losing 2-0 against Dunheved College in Launceston. Frank Howard Grose and William Pethybridge, who had formed the team from old boys of local public schools, had been students at Dunheved.

THURSDAY 10th OCTOBER 1946

Actor, screenwriter and director Charles Dance, or, to give him his full moniker, Walter Charles Dance OBE, was born. A pupil of Widey Technical School for Boys in Manadon and, later, Plymouth College of Art, Dance's big breakthrough as a thespian came in 1984 when he was cast as Guy Perron in the TV adaptation of Paul Scott's *The Jewel in the Crown*. He has appeared in many films including, early in his career, the 1981 James Bond movie *For Your Eyes Only* as evil henchman Claus.

SATURDAY 10th OCTOBER 1936

Home Park has never hosted as many football fans for a league game as the 43,596 who passed through the turnstiles to see the Pilgrims draw 2-2 with Aston Villa. Sammy Black and John Connor scored for Argyle, who had to come from behind twice and to play more than an hour of the game with only ten fully fit men after defender Harry Roberts was injured.

MONDAY 11th OCTOBER 1830

Edmund Kean, one of the greatest of English tragic actors – as well as one of the most megalomaniacal – and a specialist in Shakespearean villains, gave a special performance at Plymouth's Theatre Royal. As the advanced publicity had it: 'Being the last night Mr Kean will ever perform in Plymouth, it has been deemed expedient, for the better amusement of his patrons, to follow the plan he adopted in London, of performing his three principal characters, in three acts of different plays, in the following order: the fourth act of *The Merchant of Venice*, Shylock – Mr Kean; the fourth act of *The Dramatist*; the second act of *The Iron Chest*, Sir E Mortimore – Mr Kean; the *Farce Of The Day After The Wedding*; the fifth act of *A New Way To Pay Old Debts*.'

FRIDAY 11th OCTOBER 1957

Multi-BAFTA Awards nominee Dawn French was born. The comedienne, best known for starring in and writing *French and Saunders* alongside Jennifer Saunders and for the lead role of Geraldine Granger in the sitcom *The Vicar of Dibley*, was educated at St Dunstan's Abbey School on North Road West. French and Sunders might never have become one of the most successful comedy duos of the modern era had first impressions counted for anything: Saunders thought French was a 'cocky little upstart', while French deemed Saunders to be snooty and aloof. Dawn's mother Roma French was awarded an Honorary Doctorate from Plymouth University in 2010 for her work with the Trevi House residential rehabilitation centre for female drink and drug addicts, and Hamoaze House, a day-support centre for people with drug and alcohol problems.

MONDAY 11th OCTOBER 1869

William Taylor, a private in the 57th Rifle Regiment at Raglan Barracks, Devonport, was hanged at Exeter Gaol after a spectacular fall-out with his drill corporal. Taylor, 24, had taken exception to being told to report for extra drills and arrived on the square without his knapsack. When he was told to get his kit on by Corporal Arthur Skullen, Taylor put his rifle down and walked off. When Skullen told him to pick up the weapon, he did, took it back to the barrack-room, loaded it, walked back out on to the drill square, and shot the 35-year-old drill corporal through the head.

THURSDAY 12th OCTOBER 1944

Television presenter Angela Rippon was born in Plymouth. The daughter of a Royal Marine, she did not see her father until 1947, when he finally returned from service in World War II. After stints in the photographic department at the *Western Morning News* and with the *Sunday Independent* and BBC local radio, she joined Westward Television as an editor. However, it was back at the BBC in September 1966, that she was first seen as a presenter. By 1974, she was reading the news on national prime-time although, contrary to perceived wisdom, she was not the first female to do so – ITN's Barbara Mandell did on the second night of ITV in 1955, and Nan Winton was the first to do so on the BBC, five years later.

WEDNESDAY 13th OCTOBER 2010

A First Great Western train pulled into Paddington having left Plymouth less than two and three-quarter hours earlier, setting a new record for the fastest time from Plymouth to the capital. The special non-stop train, carrying 50 invited passengers, reached Paddington in two hours 43 minutes and 24 seconds – around 17 minutes quicker than the usual time.

WEDNESDAY 14th OCTOBER 1914

The First Canadian Division entered Plymouth Sound on their way to a four-month camp on Salisbury Plain. The Expeditionary Force of around 1,400 officers and 29,000 other ranks comprised men who were mainly volunteers with little or no military training. The First's arrival in Devonport had been so strictly censored that the fleet was completely unexpected. However, the word quickly got out and Plymothians flocked to the waterfront so that, when the Canadian troops disembarked, they marched through the streets to a warm welcome. Among their number was a doctor, Major John McCrae, of Ontario, who later wrote the poem *In Flanders Fields*. In it, he refers to the poppy fields in the disturbed earth of the Flanders battlefields and cemeteries where war casualties were buried. The poem is often part of Remembrance Day solemnities in Allied countries, while the poppy remains its definitive symbol.

SUNDAY 15th OCTOBER 1944

Western Morning News staff returned to Plymouth after more than three years producing the daily morning newspaper from Tavistock. Publication and distribution of the paper continued uninterrupted during World War II, despite the blitz of April 1941 when the paper had to be printed in Exeter.

FRIDAY 16th OCTOBER 1891

Blackadon Asylum, Bittaford, was opened by Mayor of Plymouth John Bond. Plymouth was one of the last authorities to meet its obligations to the mentally ill under the bluntly titled Lunacy Act of 1890. Previously, the borough had maintained 'lunatics' in the local workhouse, or sent patients away to places like St Lawrence's Hospital, Bodmin. By 1950, the NHS had taken over the running of the hospital, which was now known as 'Moorhaven'. It closed in 1993 and was converted into accommodation for the residents of Moorhaven village.

MONDAY 16th OCTOBER 1939

The 1,000-seater State Cinema at the junction of Victoria Road and Stirling Road opened. It was the first cinema in Plymouth to be fitted with a four-channel stereophonic system and debuted with *That Certain Age*, starring Deanna Durbin. The State became 'The Mayflower' in 1970.

TUESDAY 17th OCTOBER 1780

Porcelain pioneer William Cookworthy died and was later buried in the family vault in the Westwell Street Burial Gound. Cookworthy's feat of clay was to produce the country's first hard-paste porcelain goods, which he did by replicating classical processes used in China. A chemist with premises in Notte Street that remained in the family until 1974, he found the China clay he needed across the Tamar, established the Plymouth China Works, and started producing fine tea services, jugs and vases. Cookworthy's china was a huge improvement on existing earthenware, better than any that had previously been available anywhere in Europe. The China House pub on Sutton Harbour is said to have been one of Cookworthy's early factories.

THURSDAY 18th OCTOBER 1928

Plymouth was granted city status by King George V. The previous year, a Royal Commission on Local Government raised the question of which towns were entitled to be called cities, and wrote to the Home Office to seek clarification. The Home Office replied: "The title of a city which is borne by certain boroughs is a purely titular distinction. It has no connexion with the status of the borough in respect of local government and confers no powers or privileges. At the present time and for several centuries past, the title has been obtained only by an express grant from the Sovereign effected by letters patent; but a certain number of cities possess the title by very ancient prescriptive right. There is no necessary connexion between the title of a city and the seat of a bishopric, and the creation of a new see neither constitutes the town concerned a city nor gives it any claim to the grant of letters patent creating it a city." Once the answer had been deciphered, Plymouth submitted an application for city status, to which the King agreed. He also indicated that he had "come to an end of city making", and Southampton's application the following year was turned down.

TUESDAY 19th OCTOBER 1982

Home Park hosted its lowest-ever crowd for a league game. Just 2,525 saw Plymouth Argyle beat AFC Bournemouth 2-0 in a Third Division game with goals from Kevin Hodges and John Sims.

THURSDAY 20th OCTOBER 1853

The importance of Plymouth as a 19th-century port for imports can be seen by a report in the *Plymouth and Devonport Weekly Journal.* In just one week, Sutton Harbour and the Great Western Docks at Millbay welcomed: cattle from France, raisins from Spain, cheese from Holland, wheat from Denmark and Prussia, timber from Russia, Norway and North America, and hides from Argentina.

MONDAY 20th OCTOBER 1890

Walter Yeo, who is believed to be the first person to benefit from plastic surgery, was born in Plymouth. Yeo was brought up by his mother – an alemaker at the Royal William Victualling Yard – after his naval father died when HMS *Serpent* sank three weeks after Walter's birth. Despite this, Yeo enlisted into the Senior Service and rose to the rank of Warrant Officer in June 1917. In 1916, during the Battle of Jutland, he sustained terrible facial injuries, including the loss of upper and lower eyelids. He was admitted to Plymouth Hospital while waiting for a place at Queen Mary's Hospital in Sidcup, Kent, where he was treated by Sir Harold Gillies, who grafted skin from undamaged areas of Yeo's body across his face and eyes – a 'tubed pedicle' flap. By the summer of 1919, he was fit for active service again. Yeo died in Plymouth in 1960.

SATURDAY 21st OCTOBER 1854

Sir Thomas Martin, Tory Member of Parliament for Plymouth between 1818 and 1832, died. Sir Thomas served as Second-in-Command at Plymouth Command between 1812 and 1814 and was made Comptroller of the Navy in 1816, becoming an outspoken critic of attempts by Earl Grey's Whig government to reduce the Senior Service's budget. Grey ultimately appealed to Martin's old friend King William IV for help and Martin was dismissed in 1831. Nevertheless, Martin is credited with modernising the Royal Navy, converting the fleet from the huge battle fleets of the Napoleonic era to an effective force for colonial and commercial expeditions and defence.

THURSDAY 22nd OCTOBER 1931

The Beacon Castle Greyhound, Whippet and Sports Ground in Lipson opened for racing on Tuesday, Thursday and Friday evenings and Saturday afternoons. Admission was sevenpence. There were also trials every Wednesday evening.

THURSDAY 23rd OCTOBER 1986

The Gdynia Fountain in the centre of the St Andrew's Cross roundabout in Royal Parade was switched on by Cezary Ikanowicz, the Polish Consul General, and Bill Glanville, the Lord Mayor of Plymouth. The fountain is symbolic of the city's links to the Polish city of Gdynia, with which it had twinned ten years earlier. The main jet of the fountain can reach 30 feet high but, like the rest of the water-display, is governed by a device which reduces its height in strong winds to prevent cars and pedestrians from being soaked.

TUESDAY 24th OCTOBER 1961

The Tamar Road Bridge opened to traffic, having taken two years and three months to complete at a cost of £1.5m, with up to 300 men having worked on the structure. The first vehicle across at around 5.30am was, not a milk float, but a Western National number 76 bus on its way to Callington.

THURSDAY 25th OCTOBER 1951

Sir John Astor was elected Conservative Member of Parliament for Plymouth Sutton. 'Sir Jakie', the fourth son of Lord Waldorf and Lady Nancy Astor, both previously Plymouth Sutton MPs, tried to win the seat that had been in his family for 27 years, 18 months earlier after a distinguished record in World War II but had to wait to gain the trust of the electorate. Away from politics, he was a leading racehorse owner-trainer who had two classic winners, including 1981 St Leger winner Cut Above, which trounced the legendary Derby winner Shergar.

SUNDAY 26th OCTOBER 2003

Air Southwest took to the skies from Plymouth City Airport for the first time. Air Southwest had moved to fill a void after British Airways had announced that it was pulling out of the Newquay-Plymouth-Gatwick route earlier in the year.

SATURDAY 26th OCTOBER 1822

Richard Weymouth, a Baptist bible scholar who made one of the major 20th-century translations of the New Testament into modern English, was born in Devonport. After being educated at University College London, he entered the teaching profession and rose to become headmaster of Mill Hill School. He retired to devote himself to biblical study and to textual criticism of the Greek New Testament. The most notable of his publications was The New Testament in Modern English, a version that ordinary people could read, which was first published in 1903, a year after his death.

SATURDAY 27th OCTOBER 1928

Actress Eileen Hicks was killed while on a theatrical tour in Plymouth. The 20-year-old had been a passenger in a car driven by Samuel Martin which ran into a lamp standard in the early hours of the morning. Martin and all three passengers were injured, with Hicks dying the following day. As a result, Martin, 21, of Alexandra Road, was charged with unlawfully and feloniously causing her death. Four days later, he was remanded on a bail of £200 after a hearing at Plymouth Police Court, where it was alleged he had been driving in a reckless manner.

TUESDAY 28th OCTOBER 1902

Charles Graham was ordained as Roman Catholic Bishop of Plymouth, the city of his birth. He retired on March 16th 1911 and took the title Bishop of Tiberias in partibus. He died, Bishop Emeritus of Plymouth, on September 2nd 1912, aged 77.

WEDNESDAY 29th OCTOBER 1947

The Western end of Royal Parade, from Courtenay Street to Westwell Street, was opened by King George VI, who visited Plymouth with Queen Elizabeth to officially inaugurate the post-World War II reconstruction of the city. While in Plymouth, the King and Queen unveiled a replica of Drake's Drum at the base of the Civic Flagstaff and formally named Royal Parade and Armada Way. It is believed that when the real drum in Buckland Abbey – 'Drake's Drum' – is heard, England is under threat.

SATURDAY 30th OCTOBER 1886

Plymouth Argyle recorded their first win, in their third game, a 2-1 victory over Plymouth College. The victorious line-up was: Gale, Lumm, Baker, Lew, Grose, Chapman, Dyer, Pethybridge, Boolds, Cornish, Vaughan. Grose and Chapman scored the goals.

FRIDAY 31st OCTOBER 2008

Plymouth police took to the streets in Operation Everest, to crack down on crime on the busiest policing day of the year. Child sexual abuse warrants were executed and there were visits to dangerous offenders: a Trojan bus was used for covert patrols in relation to anti-social behaviour and criminal damage; and CCTV targeted drug activity in the city centre and Stonehouse. There were Pubwatch visits with a drug detecting dog, and an alcohol test purchasing operation.

NOVEMBER

SATURDAY 1st NOVEMBER 1958

The Reverend John Allen James, vicar of Charles with St Luke, dedicated the remains of Charles Church. Named after King Charles I, who gave permission for it to be built, Charles Church is the second most ancient parish church in Plymouth and was an important centre of spiritual life for the city for 300 years. On the night of 20th-21st March 1941, Vennel Street was hit in the Luftwaffe blitz and Charles Church was completely gutted by fire. The congregation moved to a temporary home at St Matthias and, when peace came, the ruins were allowed to remain as a 'silent shrine of remembrance' to Plymothians who died in World War II. The plaque on the north wall reads: 'Charles Church Built 1641, Consecrated 1665, Completed 1708. Named in honour of King Charles I. Ruined by enemy action. 21 March, 1941. Partially restored 1952, by the City in co-operation with the Ministry of Works. The idea of restoration having been sponsored by the Old Plymouth Society, as a memorial to those citizens of Plymouth who were killed in air-raids on the City in the 1939-45 War.' The church is now in the centre of the Charles Cross roundabout and is still occasionally used for services – like University of Plymouth carol concerts and a special service of reconciliation between Germany and Plymouth in 2001.

TUESDAY 1st NOVEMBER 1983

Stuart Hibberd, the BBC's chief announcer, died, aged 90. Plymouth College-educated Hibberd joined the Beeb after serving in the Army during World War I and his authoritative voice could be heard until the mid 1960s. His announcement about George V's imminent death – 'The King's life is moving peacefully towards its close' – was his broadcasting zenith.

MONDAY 2nd NOVEMBER 1914

A Borough of Plymouth Council was elected following the formation of a new authority combining Plymouth, Devonport and East Stonehouse. Local Government Provisional Order Confirmation No. 18 had earlier paved the way for the amalgamation of the county boroughs of Devonport and Plymouth with the urban district of East Stonehouse, after which King George V had given his Royal Assent to a Local Act which ratified the formation of what became known as 'The Three Towns'.

A PLAQUE REMEMBERING THE SOMETIMES CONTROVERSIAL SIR JOHN HAWKINS, IN THE SHADOW OF ST ANDREW'S CHURCH

WEDNESDAY 3rd NOVEMBER 1680

Attorney General Sir William Jones was elected to the House of Commons as Member of Parliament for Plymouth at a by-election. Jones directed the prosecution of the victims of Titus Oates's Popish Plot in 1678, but resigned the Attorney Generalship the following year before entering the Commons. He was a prime driver of the Exclusion Bill through the Parliament, which sought to exclude King Charles II's brother and heir presumptive, James, Duke of York, from the throne of England because he was Roman Catholic. Jones was re-elected for Plymouth to the abortive parliament summoned to Oxford in March 1681 and died a year later.

WEDNESDAY 4th NOVEMBER 1987

Queen Elizabeth's yacht *Britannia* sailed again after a £22m refit in Devonport Dockyard that included replacing the teak decks, which had been worn through in places because of excessive polishing; ridding the ship of asbestos; and removing 25 tonnes of paint which had built up over the years. The 34-year-old vessel then sailed for Portsmouth, where furniture and paintings were installed before the New Year royal tour to Australia for that country's bicentennial celebration.

SUNDAY 5th NOVEMBER 1643

After an attack on Fort Stamford by Royalists, governor of Plymouth Colonel James Wardlaw took possession of the island of St Nicholas, with the castle and magazine, previously under the charge of the mayor. All the inhabitants of the town were then required to take a vow and protestation to defend the towns of Plymouth and Stonehouse 'to the uttermost'.

TUESDAY 5th NOVEMBER 1833

William Edgcumbe, Conservative Member of Parliament for Plymouth from 1859 to 1861, was born. The son of Ernest Edgcumbe, third Earl of Mount Edgcumbe, and Caroline Augusta, daughter of Rear Admiral Charles Fielding, William was known as Viscount Valletort until 1861 when he became the fourth Earl of Mount Edgcumbe on the death of his father and entered the House of Lords. The well-connected Edgcumbe was also an Aide-de-Camp to Queen Victoria from 1887 to 1897; Lord-Lieutenant of Cornwall between 1877 and 1917; a Member of the Council to the Prince of Wales from 1901 to 1917, and Keeper of the Seal of the Duchy of Cornwall from 1907 to 1917.

MONDAY 6th NOVEMBER 1620

William Butten became the only passenger to die during the *Mayflower*'s historic journey from Plymouth to the New World, three days before land was sighted. Butten had been a servant to Dr Samuel Fuller, and fellow passenger William Bradford recalled his passing in a journal. He wrote: "It pleased God before they came half seas over, to smite this young man with a grievous disease, of which he died in a desperate manner, and so was himself the first that was thrown overboard."

MONDAY 7th NOVEMBER 1966

Gunnislake railway station became a terminus, the Plymouth, Devonport and South Western Junction Railway service to Callington having closed the previous Saturday, which also meant the demise of Chilsworthy, Latchley, Luckett and Callington Stations. The Plymouth-Gunnislake 'Tamar Valley Line' is a community railway supported by the Devon and Cornwall Rail Partnership. Six pubs in Gunnislake take part in the Tamar Valley Line rail ale trail (easier to say before going on it, than after).

MONDAY 8th NOVEMBER 1943

The United States Naval Advanced Amphibious Base was established at Queen Anne's Battery, Coxside, to prepare American servicemen and women for the D-Day landings. The 29th and 81st US Construction Battalions built a ship-repair yard; a dry dock; and three marine rail tracks. The extensive base extended to: Victoria Wharf, Martin's Wharf, Commercial Wharf, Baltic Wharf, Cattedown Quarry, Pomphlett Quarry, Shapter's Field, Richmond Walk, Turnchapel, Efford, Manadon, Vicarage Road, the old Stonehouse police station, Saltash Passage, the grounds of Saltram House, Edinburgh Street at Devonport, Coypool Depot at Marsh Mills, Chaddlewood, Raglan Barracks, the Brickfields, Devonport Park, land at Fore Street, and at HMS Raleigh and Barn Pool, at Torpoint, Plasterdown Camp, near Tavistock, and Saltash.

TUESDAY 8th NOVEMBER 1921

The Royal Marine Memorial was unveiled by Earl Fortescue, the Lord-Lieutenant of Devon, on the Royal Citadel. It comprises a bronze figure of St George, armed with a dagger, on either side of which are stone figures; *Per Mare*, a Royal Marine peering out from a hand shading his eyes and *Per Terram*, a Royal Marine leaning on his rifle.

THURSDAY 9th NOVEMBER 1843

The lighthouse on the western end of Plymouth Breakwater was finished. It is built of white Cornish granite and rises to 126ft high, 75 of which are above the top of the Breakwater. The lantern is visible for eight miles. The other end has a beacon, a metal sphere six feet in diameter mounted on a pole 20 feet above the high-water mark. It is a lifesaving device as wrecked sailors caught in high waves on the low-lying breakwater can climb into it.

THURSDAY 9th NOVEMBER 1620

After a two-month voyage from Plymouth aboard the *Mayflower*, the Pilgrim Fathers sighted the New World, at Cape Cod. Two days later, they anchored at Provincetown where, before landing, the men in the group signed the 'Mayflower Compact', an agreement to set up a council to run the colony. One of the youngest members of the colony was a baby boy born, en voyage, to Elizabeth Hopkins. He was christened 'Oceanus'.

MONDAY 9th NOVEMBER 1896

The Palace of Varieties, in Union Street, briefly became Plymouth's first cinema when film pioneer Robert Paul showed off his 'Theatrograph' in St James's Hall. The Theatrograph was the first commercially produced 35mm film projector to be produced in Britain.

MONDAY 10th NOVEMBER 1941

Lord Waldorf Astor was elected Lord Mayor of Plymouth for the third successive year. He was appointed in 1939 without even being a member of the city council, an honour given before only to Sir Francis Drake. Lord Astor held office until 1944, when Henry Mason took over.

SATURDAY 10th NOVEMBER 1810

George Legge, who stood for Parliament in Plymouth in 1778 and was elected for a two-year term, died. The elder brother of Admiral the Hon. Sir Arthur Legge and the Hon. Edward Legge, Bishop of Oxford – there is a smashing pair of Legges – George was a popular chap. After vacating his Plymouth seat, he was returned as MP for both Horsham and Staffordshire... in the same election. He chose to represent the latter.

THE ROYAL CITADEL DOMINATES THE EASTERN END OF PLYMOUTH HOE

THURSDAY 11th NOVEMBER 2010

The centre of Plymouth was evacuated following the discovery of an unexploded bomb in Notte Street. The World War II device was unearthed on the site of a former NAAFI building that was being demolished to make way for student flats. Police cordoned off an area including the Guildhall, the Holiday Inn and Tanners Restaurant, and evacuated residents were taken to Plymouth Pavilions until the all-clear was given.

THURSDAY 11th NOVEMBER 1909

The Millbay Rinkeries was opened in West Hoe Road. It comprised two roller-skating rinks and was capable of hosting 1,000 skaters on its 36,000 square foot maple-wood surface. It opened on the second wave of a craze that had begun in the 1870s and saw Plymouth boast no fewer than nine rinks, including one on Plymouth Pier. The last closed in 1987.

WEDNESDAY 12th NOVEMBER 1975

Plymouth darts player Cliff 'Ticker' Inglis earned a place in the *Guinness Book of Records* when he threw a 19-dart 1001 game, smashing all previous records. Finishing and ending on double-20, Inglis's three-dart scores were 160-180-140-180-121-180-40, which works out at an average of 52.68 points per dart, or 158.05 for each three-dart visit to the oche. Inglis's career high-spot was winning the 1974 inaugural Phonogram World Masters. The following year, he was a Unicorn World Darts Championship finalist.

WEDNESDAY 12th NOVEMBER 1595

Admiral Sir John Hawkins, shipbuilder, naval administrator, merchant, navigator, chief architect of the Elizabethan navy, Vice-Admiral alongside second cousin Francis Drake in the battle in which the Spanish Armada was defeated, and freeman of the city of Plymouth, died. In the debit column, Sir John is widely acknowledged to be the pioneer of the English slave trade. Almost four-and-a-half centuries after his death – probably from dysentery while treasure-hunting off Puerto Rico – his descendant Andrew Hawkins publicly apologised for his ancestor's actions. Born in Kinterbury Street, John's father, Captain William Hawkins, was one of the richest men in Plymouth, possibly the result of the dissolution of the monasteries, and was Mayor between 1532-33 and 1538-39. John's brother, also called William, was also Mayor between 1567 and 1568.

THURSDAY 12th NOVEMBER 1439

Plymouth came into being when a Royal Licence from King Henry VI giving his assent to a petition by townsfolk to free them from monastic rule by the monks of Plympton Priory was confirmed by an Act of Parliament. Plymouth (or what was to become Plymouth – as the higher parts of the Plym estuary silted up and ships used the Cattewater moorings and tidal harbour at the Plym's mouth, instead of Plympton, the name of the town 'Sutton' slowly became 'Plymouth') thus became the first town to achieve municipal independence by being incorporated by Parliament. William Keterigge was the first Mayor appointed by the King.

WEDNESDAY 13th NOVEMBER 1963

The Beatles played two 'houses' at Plymouth's ABC Cinema. The shows were almost cancelled after Paul McCartney came down with a case of gastric flu the day before, a situation which, before the gigs, prompted local journalist Stuart Hutchinson of Westward TV programme *Move Over Dad* ('A gay new show with the accent on the beat of the young') to ask Paul how he was doing after his reported 'collapse'. Before the Plymouth show, Paul came down with a case of the shivers, so sound engineer Ted Sparrow, of Lipson, hurried home to pick up an electric fire in the hope of preventing Paul getting any worse. While he was home, he grabbed his copy of The Beatles' first *Please Please Me* LP, which the grateful group later signed. Its value has since been estimated at £50,000. Fab. Or gear, even.

SUNDAY 14th NOVEMBER 1847

Writer and Dartmoor documenter William Crossing was born in Plymouth. Crossing lived in Drake Street and went to Mannamead School, by which time he had formed an affection for Dartmoor, notably Sheepstor, Walkhampton, Meavy, and Yannadon. He is now considered one of the best authorities on Dartmoor and its antiquities, having made it the subject of his life's work. By 1870, he had started making notes about his rambles, which resulted in his *Guide to Dartmoor*, illustrated by Philip Guy Stevens and published in 1909. The hand-drawn sketches of views and rough maps of walks, together with the descriptive nature of the walks, are like those of the Wainwright Guides to the Lake District.

FRIDAY 15th NOVEMBER 1577

Sir Francis Drake set sail from Plymouth on the orders of Queen Elizabeth I to sort out the Spanish on America's Pacific coast... and got as far as Falmouth before bad weather intervened. So the party, which consisted of the *Pelican*, four other ships and 164 men, returned home for repairs before re-embarking on what would become Drake's famous voyage around the world.

SATURDAY 16th NOVEMBER 1957

Gareth Carrivick, one of the leading directors of television comedy, was born in Stoke, Plymouth, the son of a Royal Navy electrical diagnostician. Gareth attended Plymouth Grammar School and became involved in youth theatre, which led to a lifetime in theatre and television production. He worked on such small-screen shows as *Comic Relief, The Vicar of Dibley, Two Pints of Lager and a Packet of Crisps, The Smoking Room* and *Beautiful People*, before making his feature-film debut with the science fiction comedy *Frequently Asked Questions About Time Travel*. He died of complications from a stem-cell transplant in 2010, aged 52.

SATURDAY 16th NOVEMBER 1940

Home Park hosted a special football match between the Royal Navy and the Army in front of about 8,000 spectators in aid of the Earl Haig Poppy Fund. The kick-off was performed by the wife of Lieutenant Robert Davies, a Cornish soldier who had been awarded the George Cross for heroism in defusing a bomb which threatened to destroy St Paul's Cathedral two months earlier. In May 1942, Davies was court-martialled and convicted of eight charges of fraud, obtaining money dishonestly, and theft, and pleaded guilty to 13 further charges of issuing cheques without ensuring he had sufficient funds to draw on. He was cashiered on 1st June 1942 and sentenced to two years' imprisonment, reduced to 18 months following review.

MONDAY 16th NOVEMBER 1931

Charlie Chaplin appeared on stage at the Palace Theatre as part of a two-day visit to Plymouth during which he was the guest of Lady Astor, who was also hosting aviatrix Amy Johnson and Irish playwright George Bernard Shaw. Immediately after his curtain-call, Charlie left Plymouth by the midnight train to London for the premiere of his film *City Lights*.

FRIDAY 17th NOVEMBER 1665

Sir Bernard de Gomme received his commission from Charles II to build a new citadel in Plymouth. Ever since, the Royal Citadel has dominated the eastern end of Plymouth Hoe. The stone used to build it was taken from a quarry at the opposite end, West Hoe Park. The Citadel included a small harbour, now the site of the Royal Corinthian Yacht Club, where small ships could be loaded under cover of guns of the lower fort. In later years, the Citadel became home to 29 Commando Regiment, Royal Artillery – part of 3 Commando Brigade. In 1996, during the celebrations of the regiment's centenary in the Citadel, the honorary Freedom of the City of Plymouth was conferred on the regiment.

THURSDAY 18th NOVEMBER 1897

BBC Radio presenter Derek Ivor Breashur McCulloch, better known as 'Uncle Mac' from *Children's Favourites* and *Children's Hour*, was born in Plymouth. Before joining the Beeb, he served in 16th Middlesex Regiment during World War I, and was seriously wounded at the Battle of the Somme. He lay in 'no-man's land' for three days and nights in a shell-hole 20 yards from the German lines after losing an eye and, subsequently, a lung. He joined the BBC in 1926 as an announcer and was the commentator on the first radio broadcast of the FA Cup Final the following year. He took charge of *Children's Hour* in 1933, saying: "Nothing but the best is good enough for children... our wish is to stimulate their imaginations, direct their reading, encourage their various interests, widen their outlook and inculcate the Christian virtues of love of God and their neighbours." Not *Dick and Dom in da Bungalow*, then. By 1939, the audience had reached four million, but McCulloch's health – he also lost a leg in a road accident in 1938 – was against him. Nevertheless, he presented the much-loved music request programme for children, *Children's Favourites*, on Saturday mornings from 1954 to 1965. It continued after his retirement and the programme matured into the equally successful *Junior Choice*. Uncle Mac died in 1967. Goodnight children, everywhere.

TUESDAY 19th NOVEMBER 1985

Christopher Budd was elevated to the episcopacy as the eighth Roman Catholic Bishop of Plymouth, 23 years after being ordained as a priest.

SATURDAY 20th NOVEMBER 1762

The first patients were admitted to the Royal Naval Hospital, Stonehouse, which had been built on 'No Place Field' on the southern edge of Stonehouse Creek. It was structured around a large quadrangle and took four years to construct. The nearby No Place Inn closed in 2010.

SATURDAY 20th NOVEMBER 1982

The city of Plymouth welcomed home the Falklands War Task Force. Each of the armed forces was represented in a march along Royal Parade. There was also a fly-past of many of the different aircraft that had seen service in the Falklands.

SATURDAY 21st NOVEMBER 1931

The Regent Cinema in Frankfort Street was opened. Boasting seating for 3,254 people, it was the largest in the country and one of the ten largest in Europe. Opening-night fare was *City Lights*, starring Charlie Chaplin, who had been in the city five days earlier, having arrived from New York on the *Mauretania*. As well as films, the Regent went on to host Glenn Miller & His Orchestra, and General Montgomery even used the venue to address troops stationed in the area.

SATURDAY 22nd NOVEMBER 2003

Plymouth-born rugby player Trevor Woodman helped England win the World Cup for the first and only time. The loose-head prop forward went to Liskeard School in Cornwall and represented Cornwall Under-16s before playing for Plymouth Albion. He moved to Bath, and then on to Gloucester, and won his first England cap in 1999. It was another three years before he made his first international start, against New Zealand, and he timed his run into England's 2003 World Cup team in Australia to perfection, sealing his place in coach Clive Woodward's starting XV through strong performances in pre-tournament matches.

TUESDAY 23rd NOVEMBER 1824

Much of the south-west coast was devastated by hurricane winds and the attendant abnormal rise in sea-level and huge waves, including Plymouth Breakwater. The sea defence had 200,000 tons of stone removed from it by the elements, which were also responsible for sinking 22 vessels in Plymouth Harbour.

TUESDAY 24th NOVEMBER 1908

Edith Kent, the first woman in Great Britain to be given equal pay to men, was born in Plymouth. Edith was the first female employed at Devonport Dockyard when, in 1941, she took a job as a welder on pay of £5 and six shillings a week. At 4ft 11in, she was small enough to weld in places, such as torpedo tubes, that her male colleagues could not reach, and she was so good she was soon on a higher wage than the average for a male manual worker – unheard of at the time. "It made me a bit uncomfortable that I was the first woman to earn the same as the men," she said, "and in some cases I was earning more than them. All the men I worked with were marvellous and they didn't seem to mind me earning the same." When World War II finished in 1945 and the male workforce returned from the front, she became a barmaid.

FRIDAY 25th NOVEMBER 1825

Plymouth Bank shut the tills, pulled down the shutters, and closed its doors for the last time, 52 years after it had opened in Great Broad Street under the name of Messrs Baring, Lee, Sellon and Tingecoombe. John Baring Junior and his three partners had also previously opened the Devonshire Bank in Exeter and were also involved in banking in London. His brother Francis developed the London banking firm into Baring Brothers, made famous in 1996 by Nick Leeson's inventive approach to high finance.

WEDNESDAY 25th NOVEMBER 1942

Archbishop of Canterbury William Temple opened the St John's Community Centre in Duke Street, Devonport.

SATURDAY 26th NOVEMBER 1904

The first burial took place at Weston Mill Cemetery, which was later to become one of the largest sites of Commonwealth war graves in the country. The cemetery contains 398 burials from World War I and another 556 from World War II, 12 of which are unidentified. The cemetery's garden of remembrance was built in 1949 by the City Engineer's department in stone taken from municipal buildings destroyed in the blitz of 1941.

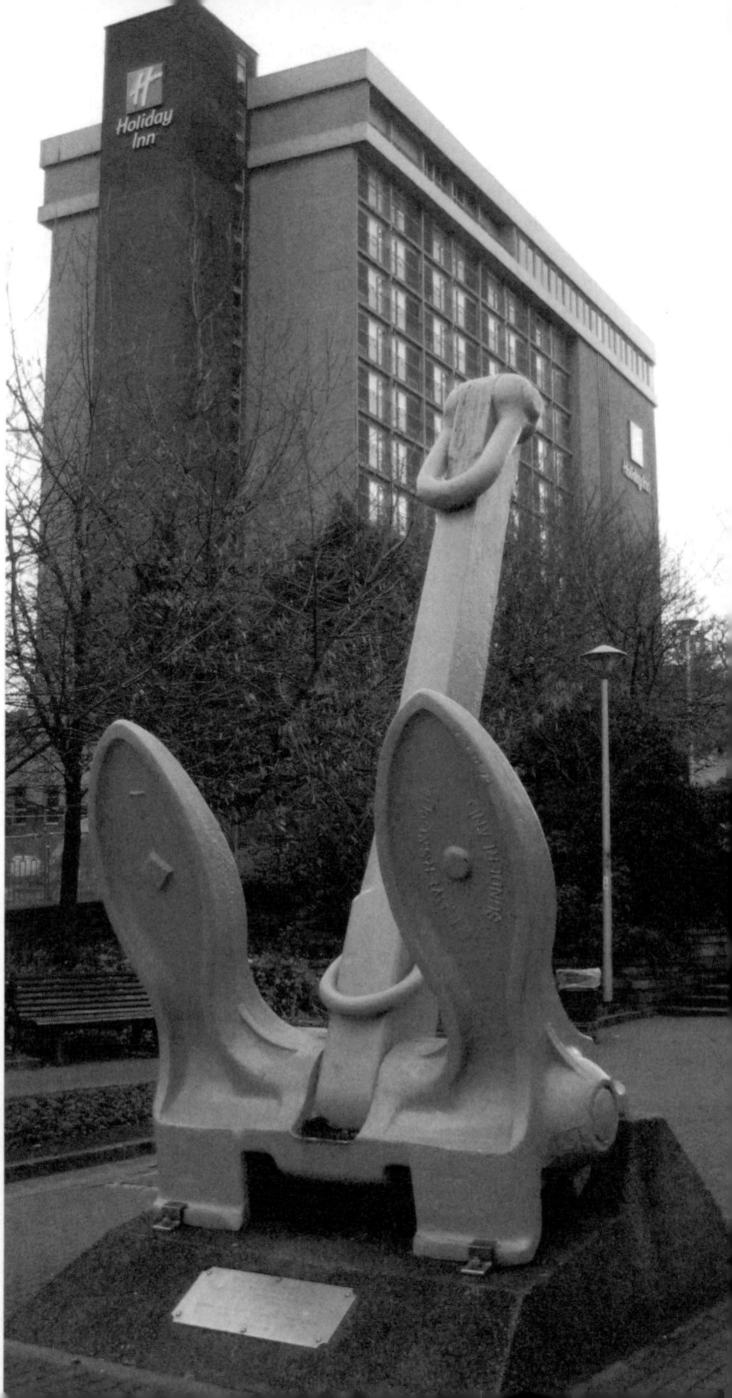

ONE OF HMS *ARK ROYAL*'S ANCHORS, IN NOTTE STREET

THURSDAY 27th NOVEMBER 2008

The Letters Patent granting Arms to the University of Plymouth were presented by Eric Dancer, Lord-Lieutenant of Devon, in a ceremony at the University. The arms contain: books, representing learning and scholarship; small stars, representing navigation; and scallop shells in gold, representing pilgrimage. A pelican and a golden hind – the original and more popularly recognised names of Sir Francis Drake's famous vessel – support the shield. The crest contains the Latin motto Indagate, Fingite, Invenite which translates as 'Explore, Dream, Discover', a quote from Mark Twain that reflects the university's ambitions for its students and Plymouth's history of great seafarers.

FRIDAY 28th NOVEMBER 1913

Plans to amalgamate Plymouth, Devonport and East Stonehouse began in earnest when the Common Seal of the Mayor, Aldermen, and Burgesses of the Borough of Plymouth was appended to the Local Government Board asking for the authority to join the borough of Plymouth, the borough of Devonport, and the urban district of East Stonehouse into one.

SUNDAY 29th NOVEMBER 2009

Bishop of Exeter the Right Reverend Michael Langrish bestowed the title of 'Minster' on St Andrew's Church. The title has only ever been granted to a handful of other churches across the country – and it made St Andrew's the only Minster in the Diocese of Exeter. The announcement followed a petition by Plymouth City Council which noted the 'remarkable inspiration' of the church's famous Resurgam motto during World War II and resolved 'to request the Bishop of Exeter to grant our historic Civic Church of St Andrew the style and title of Minster, in recognition of the very great esteem in which this Church and its record of service is held by the City of Plymouth'. The title of 'Minster' dates back to monastic times when it was used to describe a major centre of Christian mission. Speaking in a radio broadcast in 1946, politician Isaac Foot spoke of St Andrew's as Plymouth's 'most treasured possession'. He said: "St Andrew's is at the very heart of the city. Plymouth and St Andrew's have, in a sense, grown up together and the church is regarded as the common inheritance of the people, irrespective of their religious persuasion.'

SATURDAY 30th NOVEMBER 1957

St Andrew's Church, the largest parish church in Devon, was re-consecrated (on, appropriately, St Andrew's Day), following post-World War II re-roofing and restoration work by Frederick Etchells. St Andrew's had been restored twice before; in 1824 by John Foulston, and by Sir George Scott in 1875.

DECEMBER

MONDAY 1st DECEMBER 1919

Nancy Astor became the first woman to take her seat as a Member of Parliament after winning a by-election for the Conservatives in Plymouth Sutton. Constance Markiewicz had been the first woman elected to the House of Commons in the General Election a year earlier but, in line with Sinn Féin's abstentionist policy, she did not take her seat. She was also in Holloway Prison at the time. Astor succeeded her second husband, Waldorf Astor, who had been elevated to the peerage. She represented the ward for nearly 26 years, although her tenure was not without controversy, most notably during World War II, when perceived Nazi sympathies saw her dubbed 'The Honourable Member for Berlin'. She is alleged to have enjoyed several exchanges with Prime Minister Winston Churchill, e.g. in response to a question from Churchill about what disguise he should wear to a masquerade ball, she replied: "Why don't you come sober, Prime Minister?"

SUNDAY 1st DECEMBER 1872

Sir Edward St Aubyn, the first Mayor of Devonport, died from neuralgia, aged 73. St Aubyn was one of 15 children fathered by Sir John St Aubyn whose gifts to Devonport included a site for the town-hall, a corporation mace, and a cabinet of minerals, many of which can still be seen in the city's museum.

TUESDAY 2nd DECEMBER 1862

Historian Sir Charles Mallet, Liberal Member of Parliament for Plymouth from 1906–10, was born. Sir Charles was briefly Financial Secretary to the War Office in Herbert Asquith's government. His first success in the House of Commons was to secure a promise from the Admiralty that they would take more care over firing practice in Cawsand Bay which was endangering the lives of constituents who made a living from fishing.

TUESDAY 3rd DECEMBER 1833

The Royal William Victualling Yard was formally named, after King William IV, the 'Sailor King' and Lord High Admiral 1827-28. The yard was designed by Sir John Rennie for use by the Admiralty as a supply depot for the Royal Navy. It was closed in 1992, passed into private ownership, and has since been undergoing conversion to an upmarket mixed-use development.

SUNDAY 3rd DECEMBER 1643

The English Civil War Battle of Freedom Fields, also known as the 'Sabbath Day Fight', was won by the town's outnumbered Parliamentarians. Like other ports during the English Civil War, Plymouth sided with the Parliamentarians and so was isolated from the rest of the Royalist sympathetic Westcountry. The town was besieged almost continuously between 1642 and 1646 but was able to resist thanks to the Navy's support for Parliament which permitted supply ships, and even vessels containing reinforcements, to dock. The most significant action of the siege was a narrow victory over the Royalist cavalry along Lipson Ridge. Under Prince Maurice, the King's men had had advanced as far as the medieval walls before, as they awaited reinforcements, they were thrown back by a counter-attack led by Colonel William Gould. The hill where the battle was won is still known as 'Mount Gould'. Many of the retreating royalists were drowned in Lispon Creek as the tide had come in during the battle and blocked their escape route. The action allowed the only south-west Parliamentarian port in the war to remain open, changing the whole course of the war, and, consequently, English history.

THURSDAY 3rd DECEMBER 1959

The BBC Light Programme broadcast its long-running touring radio variety show *Worker's Playtime* from the Plymouth Guildhall, two months after it had been reopened by Field Marshal Montgomery following six-and-a-half years of restoration work. Comedian and Carry On film star Terry Scott was on the bill. June Whitfield was not.

SUNDAY 3rd DECEMBER 1944

Plymouth's World War II Local Defence Volunteers were stood down in a ceremony on the Hoe.

THURSDAY 4th DECEMBER 1913

The leader of the Suffragette movement, Emmeline Pankhurst, was arrested at Plymouth while still on board the White Star steamship *Majestic* after arrival from New York. A large crowd, including Suffragette leader Flora Drummond and a suffragist band, had gathered at the Great Western Docks, but were outwitted by the authorities who spirited Pankhurst away on board a special tender to Bull Point, the Government explosives depot. From there, a convoy of cars took her across Dartmoor to Exeter county gaol.

MONDAY 4th DECEMBER 1978

HMS *Ark Royal* entered Devonport Dockyard for the last time and was decommissioned two months later, depriving the world of the Royal Navy's last remaining conventional catapult and arrested-landing aircraft carrier. Twelve months later, Admiral of the Fleet Lord Peter Hill-Norton presented one of *Ark Royal*'s anchors to the city at a ceremony where the anchor was sited, in Notte Street.

SUNDAY 5th DECEMBER 1971

Iranian avant-garde rock guitarist Kavus Torabi was born, in Tehran, 18 months before his family moved to Plymouth. Their intended temporary stay became permanent following the Islamic Revolution in 1979 and Torabi became a student at Plymouth College. It was as a teenager in the city that he formed Die Laughing, a psychedelic/thrash metal group that existed between 1988 and 1993, with long-time friend and musical ally, and fellow Plymothian Dan Chudley. Since then, Torabi has been involved in a number of groups – including his own vehicle, Knifeworld – the most well-known of which is arguably the Cardiacs. Other projects/collaborations/acts include: The Monsoon Bassoon, Guapo North Sea Radio Orchestra, The Mediaeval Baebes, Chrome Hoof, Miss Helsinki, Admirals Hard, Authority and Hatchjaw and Bassett.

MONDAY 6th DECEMBER 1897

The first motor car seen in Plymouth started work. Bought by city centre store Spooner & Company to aid their deliveries, the London Motor Car and Wagon Company-built vehicle had taken two days to drive from the capital to the city. Plenty of time for Spooner's employee William Heath to receive a driver's crash-course, although, thinking about it, that is probably not a great expression to use. Before its first day of work, the Daimler-style car ferried interested newspaper reporters on return trips out to Yelverton Rock at a top speed of 12 miles per hour.

WEDNESDAY 6th DECEMBER 2006

Plymouth Music Zone secured £50,000 of Big Lottery funding to create the city's only multi-sensory music project for disabled children. Their idea to build a 'Sensation Music Station' was one of only eight bids selected for Westcountry Television's People's Millions vote.

THURSDAY 7th DECEMBER 1775

Sir Charles Saunders, First Lord of the Admiralty, Royal Navy Admiral during the Seven Years War, and Member of Parliament for Plymouth, died. Sir Charles commanded the fleet which successfully navigated the treacherous St Lawrence Seaway to land British general James Wolfe and thousands of troops at Quebec in Canada in 1759. He helped Wolfe win the Seven Years War's pivotal Battle of the Plains of Abraham, in which the French were defeated and lost their Canadian stronghold, by stopping supplies reaching the French garrison. Sir Charles was MP for Plymouth between 1750 and 1754.

MONDAY 8th DECEMBER 1755

Lighthouse keeper Henry Hall died at his home in East Stonehouse, after a fire at the Eddystone Lighthouse, when a spark from the lamp set the roof alight. The 94-year-old and two companions were unable to extinguish the fire, and they were forced to retreat down the tower until the lighthouse burned down to the rocks. They were rescued the next day but Hall had suffered burns from molten lead that dripped down from the burning lighthouse tower. The autopsy also revealed that he had swallowed some and that a seven-ounce shot had been removed from his stomach. There is a plaque dedicated to Hall set into the pavement in Millbay Road.

TUESDAY 9th DECEMBER 1902

Lillie Langtry starred at Union Street's Palace Theatre in *The Crossways*, which she wrote in partnership with London-born playwright John Hartley Manners. Lillie Langtry was born Emilie Charlotte Le Breton in Jersey in 1853 and was a highly successful actress before becoming better known for being the mistress of the future King Edward VII.

SUNDAY 10th DECEMBER 1786

The Danish cargo ship *Die Frau Metta Catharina von Flensburg*, loaded with hemp and leather bound for Genoa, sank during a full-scale gale in Plymouth Sound. Although the crew of captain Hans Jensen Twedt's anchored brigantine was saved, the cargo was lost. In 1973, the *Metta Catharina* was discovered by the Nautical Archaeology Society of Plymouth Sound who found that the highly-prized Russian reindeer leather had been preserved by a layer of thick silt and was still in excellent condition.

MONDAY 11th DECEMBER 1620

Having set sail from Plymouth three months earlier, the Pilgrim Fathers found a place free of Native Americans to establish their settlement – Plymouth. The place had been named some five years before the Pilgrims arrived, when Captain John Smith had mapped the coastline. It was Smith's tribute to the Virginia Company of Plymouth, a business founded in 1606 by James I with the purpose of establishing settlements on the coast of North America.

SATURDAY 11th DECEMBER 1886

'The Argyle ground – Mount Gould' staged the first Plymouth football derby when Argyle – just plain old 'Argyle' – played Plymouth United. Argyle also played at Marsh Mills before adopting 'Plymouth' as part of their name.

SATURDAY 12th DECEMBER 1807

Benjamin Newton was born in Plymouth. Originally a Quaker, he helped found 'The Providence People' as they were known after their nonconformist non-denominational place of worship, Providence Chapel in Raleigh Street. By 1845, 'the brethren from Plymouth' had more than 1,000 worshippers, which necessitated the building of an additional larger chapel in Ebrington Street. The Plymouth Brethren movement expanded into Europe and beyond, but theological differences between Newton and John Darby led to a public and undignified schism in the movement, and to Newton leaving it in 1847.

FRIDAY 13th DECEMBER 1577

Sir Francis Drake's circumnavigation of the globe began in the *Pelican*. Nearly three years later, after equal measures of discovery and piracy (mainly against the Spanish in the New World), the *Golden Hind* (née the *Pelican*) sailed back into Plymouth with Drake, 59 crew (out of an initial 164), Spanish treasure and exotic spices on board. Elizabeth I's half-share of the cargo surpassed the rest of the crown's income for the year and she also received, from Drake, a jewel of enamelled gold taken as a prize off the Pacific coast of Mexico and bearing an African diamond and a ship with an ebony hull, to mark the circumnavigation. Not surprisingly, Drake was awarded a knighthood aboard *Golden Hind*. The ceremony was performed by a French diplomat, Monsieur de Marchaumont, a sneaky move by Elizabeth to gain implicit political support of the French for Drake's anti-Spanish actions.

TUESDAY 13th DECEMBER 2005

The Right Reverend John Ford was consecrated Anglican Bishop of Plymouth in Exeter Cathedral by the Archbishop of Canterbury, Dr Rowan Williams. Bishop John, the ninth to hold the post since it was introduced in 1923, succeeded the Right Reverend John Henry Garton.

SATURDAY 14th DECEMBER 1918

Arthur Benn was elected the first Member of Parliament for the new constituency of Plymouth Drake. Benn, knighted in election year and later ennobled, had been the Conservatives' man in the seat of Plymouth before it was subdivided into Devonport, Drake and Sutton. While representing Drake, Sir Arthur was created a Baronet of Plymouth, in the County of Devon. He lost his seat in 1929 and died seven years later, when the baronetcy became extinct.

THURSDAY 15th DECEMBER 2005

OFCOM, the independent regulator for the communications industries, awarded a five-year community radio licence for Plymouth to Christian broadcasters Spirit of Plymouth. 'Cross Rhythms Plymouth 96.3FM' launched on March 29th 2007 with a dedication service and live broadcast from at St Andrew's Church attended by around 450 people, including Lord Mayor Michael Fletcher.

MONDAY 16th DECEMBER 1850

The first of the First Four Ships landed in New Zealand. The First Four Ships is the collective name given to the four... er, ships chartered by the Canterbury Association which had left Plymouth three months earlier to take the first English settlers to new homes in Canterbury, New Zealand. The four ships were the *Randolph*, the *Cressy*, *Sir George Seymour* and the *Charlotte Jane*, the last of which anchored at Lyttelton Harbour. The first of the Pilgrims to go ashore was James Fitzgerald, who was determined to start a new life Down Under after him and his wife Frances had fallen out with her father. Fitzgerald was later elected Member of Parliament for Lyttelton and represented it from 1854 and 1857 as well as serving as the first Superintendent of the Canterbury Province. After a brief interlude from national politics, he returned to the fray and founded *The Press*, which remains Christchurch's largest newspaper today – and represented Ellesmere and City of Christchurch, becoming a champion of Maori rights.

THURSDAY 16th DECEMBER 2004

HMS *Vanguard* the first of the Royal Navy's nuclear-powered Trident missile submarines to be refitted at Devonport Dockyard, left Plymouth. A dedicated dock had been built to do the work, which was part of a £5bn contract and took two years. During that time, she was the subject of a number of protests by anti-nuclear campaigners.

FRIDAY 17th DECEMBER 1954

The first television transmissions to Plymouth were made from North Hessary Tor, a hill just over 500 metres high near Dartmoor Prison, in Princetown. Programmes could be received in the city and a 20-mile radius surrounding area.

THURSDAY 18th DECEMBER 1777

Thomas Beaumont Bewes, MP for Plymouth between 1832 and 1841, was born. Son of two-time Mayor of Plymouth John Bewes, Thomas stood for Parliament in 1806 in an attempt to succeed his late father-in-law John Culme, the reform politician. Despite spending a lot of money, he was unsuccessful. Three years later, his wife died and Thomas moved into Tothill House where his spinster sister-in-law could look after the children. In 1813, Thomas married again and moved into Friary House, previously owned by Royal Navy captain Sir Michael Seymour, before buying what he eventually called 'Beaumont House' from the Manor of Sutton Pill for £750. In 1832, with the Municipal Reform Bill before Parliament, and with 30,000 people having attended a meeting on the Hoe in support of it, Bewes and wine merchant John Collier stood on the reform ticket and were returned unopposed. Bewes held his seat until 1841, when he retired, and he died at Beaumont House in 1857.

THURSDAY 19th DECEMBER 1867

Plymouth Corporation's water engineer Robert Hodge issued his report on how to implement the provisions of the Plymouth Corporation Water and Markets Act. The Act made provisions for water to be piped into domestic and commercial properties in return for a yearly rate, which enabled the corporation to make further improvements. Hodge's main recommendation was to lay pipes to replace the open Dartmoor watercourse – 'Drake's Leat' or 'Plymouth Leat' – that had carried water from the River Meavy into reservoirs at Drake's Place, Crownhill, Hartley, Roborough and Yelverton.

TUESDAY 20th DECEMBER 1988

A serious fire completely destroyed the fourth and fifth floors of Dingles department store and badly damaged the rest of the building. The blaze – the worst seen in Plymouth since the World War II blitz – was caused by a fire-bomb and was one of a series of attacks around the country on stores owned by House of Fraser. Initial damage reports were estimated at £13.2m, which was not, apparently, the aim of the never-apprehended militant animal rights activists. It was later claimed that they had wanted only 'to burn a few fur coats' and that their target had been the stock, not the building. The store was refurbished, and top two floors rebuilt by 1989.

TUESDAY 21st DECEMBER 1847

Colonel John Chard, who won the Victoria Cross for his role in the defence of Rorke's Drift during the Anglo-Zulu War in 1879, was born in Plymouth. Chard was commissioned into the Royal Engineers in 1868 and served in Bermuda and Malta before, having risen to the rank of lieutenant, being sent to South Africa. He was in charge of the supply depot at Rorke's Drift when it was attacked by Zulus, and 139 British soldiers successfully defended the garrison against an intense assault by 3-4,000 warriors, one of history's finest defences. *The London Gazette* of May 2nd 1879 noted: 'For gallant conduct at the Defence of Rorke's Drift, 22nd and 23rd January 1879. The Lieutenant-General reports that had it not been for the example and excellent behaviour of Lieutenants Chard, Royal Engineers, and Bromhead, 24th Regiment, the defence of Rorke's Drift would not have been conducted with the intelligence and tenacity which so eminently characterised it. The Lieutenant-General adds that the success must in a great measure be attributable to the two young officers who exercised the chief command on the occasion in question.' Chard was played by Stanley Baker in the film *Zulu*; Baker owned Chard's VC and Zulu War Medal from 1972 until his death in 1976.

FRIDAY 22nd DECEMBER 2006

Home Park was purchased by Plymouth Argyle from landlords Plymouth City Council for £2.7m. Five years later, following the club being placed in administration, the Council bought back Home Park for a reported £1.6m and once again leased it to Argyle.

MONDAY 23rd DECEMBER 1644

Sir Alexander Carew, second Baronet, of Antony in Cornwall, was executed after offering to surrender Parliamentarian Plymouth to Royalist forces during the English Civil War. A Member of Parliament for Cornwall, Carew was part of a committee set up to defend the port of Plymouth from Royalist forces and was made governor of the strategically vital St Nicholas' Island in Plymouth Sound. After the Royalist victory at Stratton in Cornwall and the capture of Bristol, Carew secretly contacted the commander of the Cavaliers then besieged Exeter, offering to surrender Plymouth in return for a pardon for himself. The Royalists were willing but Carew delayed and his plans were leaked by a disloyal servant. He was arrested, tried for treason by court-martial, convicted, and beheaded on Tower Hill, London.

FRIDAY 24th DECEMBER 1802

William Bryant, the Plymouth businessman who helped popularise the safety match, was born. William first went into partnership with Edward James and Francis May to produce lucifers – early, highly unstable matches – in a factory in Woolster Street. James bailed out of the company after their premises were destroyed by (you guessed it) fire, leaving Bryant and May to establish a provisions merchants business in London. They started importing new safety matches, produced in Sweden, and by 1853, Bryant & May were selling more than eight million boxes of matches per year.

TUESDAY 25th DECEMBER 1821

The Plymouth Eye Dispensary, an idea conceived by Doctor John Butter, was opened in Cornwall Street. Initially, there were only four beds for in-patients. Two years later, it changed its name to the 'Plymouth Eye Infirmary', and five years later it became the 'Plymouth Royal Eye Infirmary' after receiving patronage from HRH the Duke of Clarence, later King William IV. In 2005, Plymouth Hospital NHS Trust announced its decision to move to Derriford Hospital in 2011.

FRIDAY 26th DECEMBER 1930

Actor Donald Moffat, nominated for a Tony for Best Actor after his best-known film role of the corrupt American President in *Clear and Present Danger*, was born in Plymouth. He was the only child of Kathleen Mary (née Smith) and Walter George Moffat, an insurance agent.

TUESDAY 27th DECEMBER 1831

HMS *Beagle* set sail from her anchorage in the Barn Pool, under Mount Edgecumbe on the west side of Plymouth Sound, for a two-year expedition to South America, Tahiti and Australia that turned into a five-year trip. Its most famous passenger was 22-year-old naturalist Charles Darwin, who had been sought by the *Beagle*'s captain Robert FitzRoy, aware of the loneliness of his job, as a gentleman companion. By the end of the expedition, Darwin had made his name as a geologist and fossil collector, and the publication of his journal which became known as *The Voyage of the Beagle* gave him wide renown as a writer. Darwin spent two months in Plymouth before setting sail, while Captain FitzRoy was supervising alterations to the ship. He stayed in lodgings in Clarence Baths with John Stokes, one of the two survey officers with whom he would share a cabin on board.

SATURDAY 27th DECEMBER 1952

Plymouth Co-op opened for business in Royal Parade, having been delayed for a couple of weeks because of a plasterers' strike in the autumn.

MONDAY 28th DECEMBER 1835

An elected council took over the duties of the old corporation of Plymouth under the Municipal Corporations Act.

SATURDAY 28th DECEMBER 1996

Pete Goss, Plymouth College Old Boy and ex-Royal Marine, hit the headlines when he braved hurricane-force winds to save the life of fellow sailor Raphaël Dinelli in the 1996 Vendée Globe solo around the world yacht race in his Open 50 yacht *Aqua Quorum*. After receiving a distress call from Dinelli in the Southern Ocean, Goss immediately turned round to rescue him. He battled for two days to reach the near-dead Frenchman who had survived 48 hours in a freezing life raft. Goss became nurse to Dinelli – who suffered from hypothermia and was so stiff with cold he could not move for days – making him sweet tea and giving him physiotherapy while he made his slow recovery. Goss was awarded the MBE by the Queen, and the Legion d'Honneur by the French President, for his actions.

SATURDAY 28th DECEMBER 1940

Fourteen high-explosive bombs and about 1,000 incendiaries were dropped on the city after a respite over Christmas. The City Hospital and Greenbank Hospital were both hit.

SATURDAY 29th DECEMBER 1962

The South Devon & Tavistock Railway's Plymouth–Launceston passenger service ended in spectacular style. The last journeys on the route, which also took in stations at Marsh Mills, Plym Bridge, Yelverton, Tavistock South and Lydford, were badly affected by one of the worst snow blizzards to hit the Westcountry. As a result, the 6.20pm from Plymouth terminated at Tavistock at 12.20 the following morning, while the 7.10pm Tavistock–Plymouth was stranded at Bickleigh overnight.

THURSDAY 30th DECEMBER 1841

John Foulston, Plymouth's leading architect for a quarter of a century, died. Among other achievements for which Foulston was responsible was the creation of Union Street – built across marshland to unite the three towns of Plymouth, Devonport and East Stonehouse. His best known project was the creation of a group of buildings in Ker Street, Devonport, which comprised; a Greek Doric town hall and commemorative column, a terrace of houses in Roman Corinthian style and two houses in Greek Ionic, a 'Hindoo' nonconformist chapel and an 'Egyptian' library. In his dotage, he knocked up an elaborate water garden at his home, Athenian Cottage, Mutley, and, when he was not enjoying that, he could be found driving around in a gig disguised as a Roman chariot.

TUESDAY 30th DECEMBER 1690

The contract to build the first stone dock in Plymouth was granted after the Royal Navy indentified the need to repair and restock warships. On the recommendation of Sir Walter Raleigh, King Charles II had inspected Plymouth but it was not until he was succeeded by King William III that the Admiralty instructed John Addison, its Naval Agent at Plymouth, to draw up plans. The naval base at Devonport is nicknamed 'Guz' by ratings. This originates from the word guzzle ('to eat or drink greedily'), which is likely to refer to the swift dispatching of more than one or two glasses of beer with which seamen have traditionally celebrated being back on dry – so to speak – land.

THURSDAY 31st DECEMBER 1992

Television South West (TSW) made its final broadcast – and the last, after 31 years, from television studios in Derry's Cross, Plymouth – before handing over the ITV franchise to Westcountry. TSW, franchise-holders from January 1982, transmitted special programmes during its final hours including the final edition of *Gus Honeybun's Magic Birthdays*, and a repeat of the award-winning documentary *A Day in the Life of... Beryl Cook*. The final sign-off announcement was made by Ian Stirling and Ruth Langsford, after which transmission was switched from Plymouth to HTV Wales, in Cardiff, from where Westcountry TV transmits.